Moving on and Letting Go

A Guide To Loving Yourself Again

Joanna Albrecht

Published by Joanna Albrecht 2017

This book is designed to provide support and education about energetic, emotional and spiritual subjects. It is in no way meant to replace professional psychological assistance or any other kind of professional mental health assistance. The content of this book is the sole expression and opinion of its author. Neither the publisher nor the author shall be liable for any physical, psychological, emotional abnormal reactions. Our views and rights are the same: You are responsible for your own choices, actions, and results.

Printed in the United States
A catalog record for this book is available from the United States Library of Congress.

Photography: Argentina Leyva- www.argentinaleyva.com
Chakra image created by Erik Blanco
Book formatting services by BookCoverCafe.com

www.UnfoldingLove.com

ISBN:
978-0-692-91937-8 (pbk)
978-0-9998375-0-4 (e-bk)

This is dedicated to all those who have ever lost themselves in a relationship, to those who have forgotten who they are, and especially to those who are ready to make the transition back to wholeness and a full experience of love.

COMPLEMENTARY GIFT

Thank you so much for purchasing my book!
I would like to offer you a very special gift for taking care of your self and supporting this work in the world.

Go to my website:
www.unfoldinglove.com/specialgift
And download your gifts

Many blessings on your journey!

Acknowledgments

I'd like to thank all the romantic partners I've had throughout the years with whom I have experienced deep love and heartbreak.

The deeper sorrow carves into your heart, the more your heart can be filled with love.

~ *KAHLIL GIBRAN*

Thank you to all of my beautiful and remarkable healers and friends who have helped me come back from the darkness again and again by reminding me of who I am and holding the light of truth for me when I have forgotten: Rick, Pam, David, Kraig, Jenevie, Sarah, Cory, Nicole, Jake, Ponta, Nathaniel, Kathren, Aspen, Jon, Rob, Liz, Dima, Tino, Anne, Gabrielle and anyone else that I may have forgotten in my mind, but are still present in my heart.

Special Thanks for your inspiration: Abraham, Louise Hay, Wayne Dyer, Danielle McKinnon, Marianne Williamson, Gerald Jampolsky, Lynn Grabhorn, SARK, Barbara Brennan, Nahko Bear, Matthew Hussey, Jason Silva, Pema Chodron, and all the other Great Masters who came to this planet to teach about healing and love.

Thank you Divine Source, Divine Lover, Angels, and unknowable energetic helpers that I know are there, but I can't always feel or see. Thanks for helping even when I don't seem appreciative. Please know I love you always.

PREFACE

Welcome to the Next Step of Freedom

Thank you for being brave enough to embark upon this journey. Going through the process of *Moving On and Letting Go* is not easy. It can often feel like the scariest thing you have ever done, as though your very life is in your hands and everything is up in the air, in utter chaos.

I want you to know that everything is going to be okay. I know it may seem as if things will never be all right again, but if you stick with this program you will see that you can feel strong, clear, aligned, and balanced, even if you have never felt that way before.

You might feel lost, abandoned, and alone right now, but please allow me to take your hand and begin this journey. Know that you are safe, you are loved, and you are never alone. Remember, this is a journey, a journey that will bring you back to your own loving, connected, strong self. You don't have to do this alone: I will be guiding you every step of the way.

If you are ready to meet your strong, amazing, beautiful self, let's embrace on this new chapter of your life together.

CONTENTS

INTRODUCTION

This program is designed to help you clear out the core beliefs, energies, and attachments you might have taken on from others, and it will teach you how to take back and redirect your own energy so that you can feel complete and whole. *Moving On and Letting Go* helps you to genuinely experience your authentic self and align to your true path.

The reason I wrote this book and came up with these exercises is because I have been in this state multiple times with multiple partners. I have lost myself fully and completely in the other person, becoming dependent on their energy and their love to get me through life; clinging so hard and needing that person so much that it would drive them away and leave me feeling abandoned and a total mess. I would eventually remember to do the exercises in this program, and little by little I would find my way back to wholeness again.

After a particularly challenging breakup, I finally recognized that this pattern was happening again. I said, "That's it! I am writing a book with all of the things I do to get back to myself again: one, so I can have a quick reference guide for when it happens again; and two, maybe it can help other people going through the same thing."

There are many meditation exercises for you to use. For the greatest benefit, begin these exercises in a space free from distractions. Take a few moments to settle both your thoughts and body.

CHAPTER 1

Tools for the Journey

Explanation of Energy

Let's talk science! Richard Feynman was awarded the Nobel Prize in Physics for his contributions to quantum electrodynamics. Feynman examined the results of the *double-slit experiments*, also called *wave-particle duality*, and concluded that at the very smallest molecular level, when a photon (a measurement of light) is observed, it behaves as a particle, but when it is not being observed, it behaves as a wave. Essentially, when you are observing something, it becomes a thing, but when you are not observing it, it is free-flowing energy.

Why is this important?

Because it tells us that our thoughts affect our reality: our attention can actually change how matter behaves. The more you focus on a particular thought, the more that specific reality is solidified.

Your thoughts can be light or heavy, depending on your point of view. If you are thinking about something that pleases you and makes you happy, it can feel good to you. However, if you are thinking about something that does not match up with what is true for you, it may feel heavy or cause an unpleasant feeling. There is a part of you that is connected to a more expansive consciousness. You are experiencing this connection when you feel like everything is working out in your life, when you feel everything flowing easily and effortlessly. When things are challenging or not flowing in the ways that make you feel good, this shows you have lost recognition of this connection. It doesn't mean that the connection doesn't exist; it just means that you are not in resonance—or in synchronization—with what the more expansive part of you knows to be true. When you are in harmony with that energy, everything flows easily for you. When you are out of sync, everything becomes more challenging.

In this program, we will be working with concepts such as chakras, cords, and different kinds of energies, which will all be described in greater detail later.

Chakras and cords are a tangible way to relate with what is happening with your energy. I say tangible because if you focus on these centers and cords you will be able to feel them in some way, depending on how you experience energy. People experience the flow of energy in different ways. Some people see it, some feel it, some know it, and some even smell or taste it.

Whatever way you may experience energy flow is okay. As we go through the exercises in this book, you may translate them to fit your way of sensing energy, and if you do not know yet what is your way, don't worry, you will soon enough. One of the more fun aspects in these exercises is figuring out how you process information. You may not have ever thought about how you process energy or think about the world in this specific way, but now you get to learn *how* you learn, just by paying attention.

In the beginning, the exercises might feel weird, but as you become more familiar with the meditations and clearings they will quickly and easily become, effortless, and quite relaxing. This leads me to the issue of *comfortable* versus *uncomfortable*.

Comfortable Versus Uncomfortable

When your body is free and clear of other people's energy and you are connected to your more expansive energy, you feel comfortable, open, free, and happy. When you have thoughts, concepts, or energy that are not yours or do not resonate with your more expansive frequency, you may feel uncomfortable. It is the difference between having a big hose flowing with pure, clean water or having chunks of unwanted objects blocking up the hose and stopping the flow. The things that block the flow are other people's energy, heavy thoughts, attachment cords, and people or concepts that don't make you feel good. Once these influences are released from your energy field, you feel lighter and your energy will feel free flowing again, every time.

The interesting part about this is that sometimes you will want to hold on to the energies or attachment cords that are causing you pain. The reason is that you believe that holding on to them will somehow make you feel better.

Why do we hold on to beliefs and energies that harm us?

Here is one answer: there was a point in time when we shared our energy with another person or we embraced an idea about another person, place or belief. When we thought about this person, place or concept, we felt happy. The *reason* it made us happy is that we opened ourselves up energetically, and we were able to access our more expansive self. Because that connection with our more expansive self occurred when we were around that person or concept, we thought that they were the reason we felt so good.

The truth is that person might at one time made us feel safe and secure enough to open up to the energy that is all around us, but the feeling we experienced was not coming from them. They were not the source of the energy; rather, our experience with them allowed us to open up and feel our expanded self.

When we are open to more expansive energy, we feel what is called *Love*. It feels open, flowing, and safe, although, actually, the concept of safe doesn't really apply here, because Love is the opposite of any feelings of being unsafe. Fear, doubt, and feelings of lack can arise only when you forget your connection to more expansive energy. That is a great thing to realize because now, when you or I are in fear, doubt, or lack, we will recognize that this is a signal to come back into alignment.

We can remind ourselves, "Oh, hey, I am not feeling whole right now, what can I do to come back into alignment with my more expansive self?"

The exercises in this program will help you to do just that.

Different Frequencies of Energy

Just as there are different colors, different sounds, and different flavors, there are also different frequencies of energy. Each of them provides an experience that is recognizably different from the others.

I was introduced to energy and energy healing many years ago, sort of by accident. I was looking for a massage course and saw an ad that offered a Reiki attunement. I was not really sure what it was, so the teacher gave me an energy healing.

I lay down on a massage table and he put his hands on different parts of my body. Wherever he touched me, I felt the sensation of warmth, and I felt as if I were in a trance, somewhere between awake and asleep. After the healing was finished, he did a ritual in which attuned me to the Reiki frequency so that I could channel the energy through my hands the same way he could. He said it was like tuning into a specific radio station. I would forever be tuned into Reiki 101 and be able to run the energy through my hands whenever I called on it.

For many years, I used Reiki energy to heal myself and others, and I began to meet people who did healing with other kinds of energies. What I learned in receiving healing from others is that, even if the people doing the healing were using the same kind of healing energy, like Reiki, it felt different. These healers were using the energy of the sun, the moon, trees, planetary alignments, colors, and pretty much anything you can think of, all of which can be called upon to facilitate healing.

What makes healers different from other people who do not think that they can use healing energy?

Belief.

In the beginning, I wasn't sure if what I was doing with Reiki energy was working. But I kept working with the energy and saw tangible results, so I began to believe. When you gain experience and get positive feedback, it is hard to dispute that Reiki energy is helping people.

Right now, you might wonder if any of this energy chakra stuff works. Well, the only way to know is to give it a try. You don't really have anything to lose except for the pain and suffering of the past. If you have tried everything else, you might as well try this to see what happens. It is kind of like learning a new language. It may feel weird at first, but the more you do it the easier it will become and soon it will become second nature.

I use a few different kinds of healing energies in my meditation clearings. As I call them in you may feel them or experience them in your own individual way. The most important thing to remember is to simply relax and allow the energy to flow. Everything in this program is safe and has the highest vibration of love and light. I have created a built-in safe place that we experience together.

When I was first learning about energy healing, I was scared and cautious because it was all so new. That's why I have developed this program in the most gentle and safe way possible to ease you into the process. With each exercise that you do, you will find yourself becoming more relaxed and feeling more at ease with the process.

Chakras

Chakras are basically energetic filing cabinets and distribution centers for emotional concepts and energy. In this program, we deal with the seven main chakras. If you find you love chakra work, there are many books and programs that will take you deeper into the chakra system, and what you will learn here will be a great foundation for your studies.

You will experience your chakras in the same way you experience energy. So, if you feel energy, then you will feel the chakras; if you see, you will see; if you know, you will know. Chakras will show up differently for different people, but the basic visual appearance is of a spinning vortex of energy. Each chakra appears to be of a different color. Some say the reason for this is that they are different frequencies of energy. These frequencies can also be experienced as different feelings, or tastes, and so on.

Do chakras matter?

The reason I chose the chakra system to begin your healing journey is because when you are dealing with energy and emotions, it can often be overwhelming and hard to figure out how to start dealing with the emotional chaos. It is like seeing a town that a hurricane has ripped through: debris everywhere you look. By using the chakra system, we have a step-by-step process outlining how to go about cleaning everything up. It lends order to what might otherwise seem to be an impossible task.

Where are the chakras located and what do they do?

I am going to go into each chakra in depth further on, but I will share the basic idea here. An interesting thing to note is that each chakra has two aspects: a *front aspect* that is located in the front of our body, and a *rear aspect* located at the back of our body. The front chakra is the vortex through which we give or offer our energy out into the world, and the rear chakra is where we take in and receive energy. The rear chakra determines how we use that energy for ourselves. The crown and root chakras are complementary and work together to help us to ground and connect with our more expansive self.

The main seven chakras we are working with in this program are the following:

- **Crown**: Located at the center of the top of the head.
- **Third eye**: Located in the middle of the forehead and back of the head
- **Throat**: Front and back of the throat
- **Heart**: In the center of the chest and middle of the back
- **Solar plexus**: Located at the diaphragm and lower-middle back
- **Sacral**: Two inches below the belly button and lower back
- **Root**: At the perineum, between the genitals and the anus.

Energy Cords

When we meet someone new, we create an energy cord to them. This cord of energy is like a USB cable, plugged into their computer system. It helps us to read through their files and lets us know a little more about them. Once a cord is established, it is a two-way connection: we can read their energy and they can read ours. Energy runs through this cord, and with people who love each other it can feel quite good. The information and energy running through are nice thoughts, pleasant feelings, and good wishes. But when one person is not feeling well or is crabby, the energy running through the connection can feel uncomfortable or upsetting. There can be so much of the other person's energy running through this connection that we may wonder if it is our energy or theirs, because it can overwhelm us.

While it is fun to exchange energy with people for a while, when energetic connections linger too long they can cause unhealthy attachments and dependencies. Sometimes you may begin to use the connection you have with another for all your energy needs, which will tend to drain the other person. Interestingly enough, when you release attachment cords to another person you are free to connect to the unlimited energy that is all around you, but when you are attached to or corded to another person, you are in kind of a trance that stops you from knowing this. This may seem counterintuitive, but it is when you fully and completely detach from others that you can truly be present with them.

When you are heavily corded to someone, it is almost like a drug-induced stupor. You cannot think of anyone but them. It may feel as though your partner is the only thing that will make you feel better. You need one more fix of their energy and then everything will be all right with the world. This trance state fully and completely goes away when the cords to the other person are released. But just like withdrawing from drugs, there is a point when you must want to release, while not knowing if it will work or not. Every part of you may be telling you that holding on to this energy and this cord is the only way you will ever feel happiness again, even though you haven't been happy being connected to them in a long time. There is a leap of faith that you need to take to accomplish this break.

CHAPTER 2

Rocks on the Road to Freedom

There are a few things that may come up during the process of reconnecting with your expanded energy. I want to address them so that if you do experience them, you can handle them with ease.

If you have been feeling an intense physical, spiritual, or emotional connection with someone, there is a chance that you have created energetic attachments with them. These types of connections were formed in specific ways that were designed to make you feel safe and loved in places where previously you had not. When you begin to release the attachment cord to the person, you may feel panic, fear, sadness, or doubt. This is perfectly normal. I want you to know that these feelings—no matter how intense they are—are just coming up to be released. It's like taking the cork out of a bottle: as the cork lets go, the feelings will arise and go with it.

As champagne flows out of a bottle when the cork is pulled—first rushing out quickly and then slowing down—so it will be with you. These feelings will bubble up, sometimes intensely, but they will eventually all be released and you will feel a profound state of joy once they are all completely cleared. So, let us celebrate the release and flow of *e-motions*: energy in motion.

Let's explore some examples of thoughts that may come up.

"I can't let this person go. If I do I will be alone."

Let's be truthful: you already feel alone—but it's not for the reason that you think.

When we are ending a relationship, or even if we are still in a relationship, when we feel lonely, it is because we have given all our energy away to the other person and there is no one at home in our own body. This feeling leads us to blame our partner for not being there for us or not giving us enough attention. But if we have given all our energy away and are not paying enough attention to our own needs, no amount of energy from that other person is going to fulfill us.

The only thing that will fill our need is releasing other people's energy from our space and coming back into our own body to give ourselves the energy and love we have been longing for. The lonely feelings we are experiencing are actually our own body missing us. Our body is asking us to come home.

Our physical body needs our energy and presence. When we are focused intensely on another person, giving them our complete attention and focus for extended periods of time, we start to become depleted. We may experience sadness, loneliness, or resentment. These feelings are all coming from our own body asking us to bring our presence back to ourselves. It is fine and wonderful to give another person our presence from time to time, but when we neglect our own being too much, we feel out of balance. The way to relieve this is to bring our presence back to our body.

"I can't do this, it's not going to work. I should just wait and do it another time."

You *can* do this and it *will* work, but you need to be brave enough to do something you have never done before. I know you are afraid. I have been there. I felt like there was no way I could be strong enough to let my partner go. But I was, and you are, too. You can do this. This is your life, your strength, and your happiness.

Isn't it time you take it back?

"They are my soul mate. I can't release them. We are meant to be together."

If you are meant to be together, clearing your energy field and releasing codependent cords will not change that fact. It will just make your relationship better because you won't be connecting with your partner from an attached, needy place, but from a more open and loving place. The attachments you are clearing are not soul-based connections. They are codependent attachments created from a sense of fear or lack.

When we meet someone and we feel a strong soul connection to them, we want to keep them around, so we attach an energetic cord. This makes us feel more secure because we can feel the connection through the cord. Interestingly enough, though, if we are secure in our own connection to the Earth and our Source or Divine Love Energy, we have no need for this kind of attachment. We realize that someone is in our lives because they are meant to be there. We share things with each other, and we can feel a sense of peace with one another without being tethered. In fact, the person you are with will have a greater feeling of connection to you without the cord. People like to feel they are free to choose you, not as if they *must* be with you. The paradox is: The more untethered someone feels, the more they will want to be around you.

That can surely fly in the face of everything we have ever felt about relationships, but if you deeply consider relationships that work and are happy, this sense of freedom is present. Each person has their own grounding and follows a life path that is unique, as well as sharing their lives together. They are not so much dependent upon each other, but instead are inspiring one another to be all that they can be, to be strong in their own being. This is why, whether you are still in a relationship or you are moving on from one, it is very important to create your own sense of being grounded, whole and complete.

CHAPTER 3

Why Hold On?

Why do we want to hold on to the past, even if it's painful and not working for us?

Why do we cling so tightly to something that is holding us back and keeping us from a happier, more fulfilling relationship?

I see our eternal existence as a river. The river is moving so swiftly that we want to cling to anything familiar. It seems like the familiar is safe, and we can rest there. This is not really true, but it's a common story that we tell ourselves.

We remember a time when we *did* feel happy and safe with this person, but that was a different time. In essence, you were different people living different lives then. That time, that story line, is over now. And even if you got back together, the timeline would be different, your reasons would be different, and the story would be different. The way it once was will never exist again. Let that sink in. This moment will never happen again, which could seem sad, but think of it this way: there are so many things you have not experienced yet, with so many people you have not yet met. You had a really amazing time with one person, but there are other people and other experiences that could be even more magical and more beautiful.

When you enter into a relationship, you start to identify yourself as *the couple*. Everything you do and think becomes the experience of "we" instead of "me," so that when you are unraveling from the relationship, it feels as though you are losing yourself, the identity of who you are. You might go through what is called a "Dark Night of the Soul" because you no longer know who you are without the relationship.

This usually happens for two reasons: One is that the neurological pathways in your brain have wired together many associations with this person, and they have become integrated into every aspect of your life. Two, you are still energetically tethered to your former partner. When you untangle the energetic cords that hold you together and release the core beliefs that have been anchoring them in place, letting go is easy. Not only is it easy, but it is no longer an issue.

Why is this the case?

Because the pain you may feel when holding on is due to all the lies you are trying to maintain. Lies and attachments are some of the most painful things we can experience on this planet. If you have a thought and it is hurting you, it is a lie. There is something about that thought that is not true. When you believe something that is not true, it is painful. The truth will always set you free. The truth, even if you don't like it, will feel lighter to you than a lie.

"He doesn't love me anymore. He never loved me. I suck."

These are painful thoughts, mostly because they are not true. If you sit with them and uncover the truth, there was probably a time when he did love you, and he may even love you still, but the time of being together is over now and you are parting ways. Just because you are parting ways does not mean that the love was never there, and it does not mean the love isn't *still* there. It just means that the "being together" part of your story is ending.

When going through a breakup you may look for the most painful explanation for why it happened, but maybe the truth lies in a more loving explanation.

What if no one was wrong, no one was bad?

What if you just learned all you needed to learn from that person and it was now time to experience something new with someone else, so you both can grow in a different way with a different set of circumstances?

This program is here to help you to let go of all the beliefs that have you clinging to a past that is no longer serving you.

CHAPTER 4

Where Your Energy Goes

When you think about something or someone, you send out an energy cord to that person, place, or situation through time. How emotional you are determines how much energy is channeled through that cord and how big it grows and how strong it gets.

So, if you are thinking about something you *want* to happen, that's awesome. But what if you are thinking about someone or something you are sad about or thinking about a situation you wish would *not* happen?

Well, then you are streaming all your energy to the things you don't want. I understand how easy it is to think about the negative things that have happened or the things that could be happening or will happen in the future, but consider this: the more you think about something, the more energy you put into manifesting it.

So, if you are going to spend all your energy thinking about something, wouldn't it be better to think about something you want to bring into your life rather than something you *don't* want to bring into your life?

How much time have you actually spent thinking about things that you *don't* want to happen?

In essence, worrying is praying for something you do not want to happen.

When you find yourself obsessing about things you would rather not be thinking about, notice what you are thinking about: "*Oh, I am thinking about this again.* Time to focus on something different."

Here is an exercise to redirect your energy

Find a comfortable place to relax where you won't be distracted.

Bring your attention to the energy that exists around your body. It's ok if you have never done this before, just know that when you set your intention to bring your attention to something, it will come to you easily and effortlessly. If it seems difficult, just relax and know that everything new takes a bit of time, but eventually challenging things become second nature when you do them enough times.

Starting at the top of your head, scan your body to find where a cord is attached.

Is it coming from your head?
Your heart?
Your belly?
Take some time to really feel into this cord once you have found it.

Now as you feel into the cord, notice the flow of energy that is happening. Is energy leaving you or is it coming to you?

Are you giving energy through this cord or are you taking it? Imagine breathing all of the energy you have given this person through this cord coming back into your body through this cord. Then imagine breathing all of the energy you have taken from this person back to them. When you feel the exchange of energy is complete then notice the root of where you are holding onto whatever or whomever it is. Using your intention, loosen your grip on this cord. Unravel it and ask that it be sent back to the person it is connected to. Put your hands on your body again, using your intention, move your energy into this place. Remember, often we connect with other people to fill in places where we felt empty. When you move your energy and focus into these places, they no longer feel empty, because you are now moving yourself into them. Your body no longer feels alone.

It's challenging when you are thinking about something and obsessing about it. We can become addicted to the feeling of pain and hurt with vicious thoughts that go around and around in our head like a mobius strip. In his book *The Power of Now*, Eckhart Tolle talks about being *in the pain body*. He says that when you are in the pain body, all you want to do is focus on the things that can hurt you more and what things can hurt others more. This bringing back of the energy cord helps get you out of the pain body and back into your physical body. The more present you are in the physical body, the safer and calmer you will feel.

Here is an Exercise that will help you to connect to your own Source of Energy and groundedness

Bring yourself into a calm and comfortable space. Start breathing deeply and imagine the base of your body and legs softening downward into the Earth. Relax and breathe as you imagine the bottom part of your body taking root, like a tree into the Earth. Imagine having strong firm roots that allow you to feel safe and secure in any storm. When you are rooted nothing can shake you. You are strong safe and confident.

Once you feel very grounded and calm, focus your attention on the top of your head and imagine connecting up to the sun. Breathe up to the sun and imagine a cord of light connecting you to the light. Inhale the light and energy down from the sun into the top of your head and down into your body. Fill your whole body with a warm, deeply cleansing, and nurturing light.

Notice how you feel when you are grounded and breathing in this pure flowing continuous energy.

CHAPTER 5

Rewiring Your Brain

Are you in a trance when it comes to another person? Do you obsess about them?

Does your whole life get pushed aside because your thoughts are filled mostly with them?

Do you have trouble focusing on daily activities because they are all you can think about?

These are some of the reasons for obsession: depending on how long you have been together, your brain has formed associations with this person. Every time you were together, every place you have ever been, conversations you have had, music you have listened to, movies or shows you have watched, food you have eaten—all of these experiences and things are now associated with this person. You have trained your mind to automatically think of this person when any of these come up. The good news is you can change this. You can reprogram your mind. Just as you programmed it in the first place, you will be able to shift your focus from this person to other things and people. Here are some things that will assist you in making the shift easier.

1. **Cut off all contact.**

   You need a period of at least twenty-one days of zero interaction. No calls, texts, emails, letters, looking at old photos or stalking them on Facebook or other social media.

   Because you spent a good deal of brainpower and energy thinking about this person and your relationship, they are literally woven into the very fabric of your brain, specifically your neural pathways. When you do something new, your brain remembers it by creating new connections. The more you do something, the more connections are created, and the stronger they get. When you have been in a relationship for a while, there are many connections and associations you have with this person. You will remember them when you think of different places, situations, and people because they are entangled. Thoughts that are fired together are wired together.

   If you can give yourself twenty-one days without contact, these connections will start to loosen up and will not have the emotional charge they once did. Tara Swart, a senior lecturer at MIT, says in her book *Neuroscience for Leadership*:

   Depending on the complexity of the activity, [experiments have required] four and a half months, 144 days, or even three months for a new brain map, equal in complexity to an old one, to be created in the motor cortex. This means, if you want a new brain and to be able to think in a new way you have to be willing to give it time to rewire itself. Give it time to override the old programming so it can create something new. 21 days is the minimum to create a new habit, but for a complete brain rewiring it will take a bit longer.

2. **The biggest social media present you can give yourself is to completely block your former partner on Facebook.**
I know this sounds extreme, but in your weakest moments you are going to want to see what your former partner is doing. I will let you in on a secret: there is nothing but pain waiting for you on that page.

There is a saying, "Stop looking for happiness in the same place you lost it." I know you think that looking at their page is going to make you happy somehow, but it won't, at least not right now. You can always unblock them in the future if you want to, but for the next twenty-one days give yourself a break and a good fighting chance at sanity with a complete block. Blocking them also will keep you from seeing if they comment on anything; basically, it will stop you from seeing any trace of them on Facebook.

If you are friends with them on any other social media outlet, unfriend or unfollow them there, as well.

If for some reason you break the no-contact rule, then you need to start counting the days from day one again. You must give your brain a chance to rewire itself and that takes time. It will not happen overnight, but it will happen.

3. **Shift the flow of your energy and thoughts.**
If you find yourself thinking about or obsessing about them, stop; take a deep breath and say to yourself, "Forward thinking, present moment."

As you think about the past, you can imagine it as a stream that flows away from and behind you. As you focus your energy, you are moving your thoughts in a forward motion, into the future. This visualization will help you to move forward in your thoughts and your life. I do this when I am walking and can feel the shift as I stride forward. The more you do it, the easier it gets.

4. **Distractor!**

Just like above, another thing you can do when you notice yourself thinking and obsessing about another person or a subject you don't want to think about is to notice and then say,

"Distractor!" This will shake you out of the trance and allow you to remember to focus on what you want to focus on and not be distracted by what you don't want to be thinking about.

CHAPTER 6

Redirecting Obsessive Thoughts

When you have had a loss in your life, the tendency is to focus on all the negative things that have happened and make up stories about the negative things you did or the other person did. All this does is perpetuate the negative energy and patterns. This mindset will keep it all alive. You are sad and in pain and you want it to end, but every time you think about the things you don't want, you invite more instances of them into your life.

When you find yourself talking about the things that you wish you were not experiencing, stop. Redirect your focus.

Say to yourself: "Okay, this is what I was feeling, how do I want to feel *now*? That is what *was* happening. What would I like to be happening *now*?"

This simple shift in thought and perspective can help to move your energy and emotion in a different direction.

Negative thinking is like falling into a ditch. You can raise yourself out of the ditch, but you may sometimes stumble and fall back into it.

Negative thinking is easy because our minds have been trained to look for what is wrong so we can fix it, but what if the very act of looking for what is wrong *causes* what is wrong?

What if, because of your focus, you are actually manifesting the very things you are afraid of?

Negative thinking can be an addiction to a familiar feeling, even though it is a painful feeling. Not only that, but when we are in the pain body, as described by Eckhart Tolle, we also want to inflict pain on others. Bringing ourself into a more calm and loving place not only brings us out of the pain body it helps us to see ourselves and others in a clear light and helps us to loosen our grip over obsessive negative thoughts.

CHAPTER 7

Let Go of the Story

Your thoughts, feelings, and emotions all resonate at a certain frequency and vibration. When you tell the story of your past, you tune into that specific frequency, like a familiar radio station. This is unwanted for a number of reasons, but first, the unpleasant memories make you feel bad. Second, thoughts of the past put you in a negative mind loop in which you keep repeating the same thoughts over and over, and the energy gets stronger and stronger, like rolling a quickly growing snowball.

When this happens, you not only start resonating at the same frequency as in the past, but you actually can attract similar energy to you. This is why people tend to repeat unwanted relationships again and again. If you keep talking about the things you did not like in the last relationship, you will call them in again because you are recreating that same vibration every time you talk about it.

A part of us will always want to try to fix the past by bringing up old stories, but there is no changing what has happened. You can only shift the energy of this present moment to make sure you create a better future.

When you find yourself thinking of something that happened in the past or reliving a story, remember the saying from Chapter 5 and use it like a mantra. Say: *Present moment. Forward thinking. Or Distractor! Distractor!*

This will bring you back to this moment and shift your thought stream in a new direction. If you knew the intensity of the flow of energy you are using to think about the past, it would amaze you. When you are able to shift all that energy into the present moment and direct it toward where you would like to go, your life will move forward faster than you imagined.

Sometimes we focus on the past because we may be afraid of what comes next. The past, even if it was a crappy one, seems safer than an unknown future. If you are like most of us, though, you are afraid of the future only because you are afraid you may repeat the past. We repeat the past only if we keep thinking about it. Therein lies the cycle.

There are many organizations that advise us to "remember the past, lest we forget."

Let's consider the word *remember*: to *re-member* means to put back together something that has happened in the past.

A more productive way to create a better future begins by visualizing a better future. Think about what you want, see it clearly, and then take the steps to make it happen. The same goes for your next relationship. Visualize in your mind's eye what you would like to experience, then go one step further and bring up the feelings you would like to feel in this new relationship. Bring them up every day. Feel them as vividly as you can. Have as much fun as you can. Talk to your future partner, have fun with them, go for walks and talk to them. Imagine what it feels like to be together.

This brings you into the vibration and frequency of what you wish to create. When you are in the frequency long enough, you become a magnet for that same frequency to come into your life. Eventually a new partner won't be able to help but come in, and when they do, it will feel easy and natural, like they have been with you for a long time. In essence, you have been in each other's same energy and frequency for as long as you have been calling it to yourself.

CHAPTER 8

Energy Exchange

Before you and I incarnated into our bodies here on this planet, we were pure energy. We could feel what it was like to be one with everything. We needed only to think about someone, and we could instantly merge with a person. Being intimate with a partner in a loving way is about as close as we get to that feeling while in a body. That is why we try to hold on to that feeling as much as we can. It's why we try to continue a partnership even when we know it is not good for us. We are looking for that feeling of connection with the Divine, and although our partner might not have been the Divine, they gave us a reason to tap into that feeling.

A Breakdown of What Is Happening

Most people are not totally energetically present within their body. This can look a lot like being scattered, like not being able to think clearly or feel strong and healthy physically, emotionally, or mentally, like not loving yourself fully, disowning certain aspects of yourself, and so on. When we meet someone and engage with them in a romantic relationship, there are certain parts of their energy that fill in those missing aspects of us. This connection makes us feel complete and whole. We feel safe and happy, and when we feel complete, safe and happy we open up fully and connect to Divinity. When we are connected to Divinity, we feel like everything is a miracle, everything is working out, and we are One with everything. It awakens us and makes us feel alive.

The problem arises when we misidentify our connection with our partner as our connection with the Divine. We start to depend on our partner for that sense of belonging and connection. In truth, we all have our own connection to the Divine, but for some reason we don't remember it, don't feel worthy of it, or feel like other people have a better chance at connecting than we do, so we use our partner as a conduit for connection.

Sharing energy with your partner will work for a while. The two of you will merge in love and connect together, but eventually your partner is going to get tired or want to focus on other things. When this happens, you might get upset or feel as if you are being abandoned. You feel like your connection to the Divine is being cut off, and it is—but only in that specific pathway.

What you are learning is that your partner was not created to be your Source Energy; they were not born to be your battery. Only your own unique connection to Divine energy will permanently and consistently restore you and bring you a sense of secure well-being.

Reactivating Your Divine Connection

You can re-activate your own connection by noticing where your connection to the Divine Source is coming from by sensing your connection to the Source at the top of your head.

Is the connection going straight up?

Or is it going off to the side?

You can feel it, sense it, or know it. If you get quiet and ask, you will receive an answer. If it is going off to one side, that means you are using someone else or their connection as a pathway, instead of your own.

Take a moment to bring that connection back from that other person and redirect it to Source: straight up.

Doing this will make a huge difference in how you feel about that other person. It often takes away any fear, anxiety, and neediness you have been experiencing.

Another reason you might feel clingy or needy is if you are using the other person's grounding cord. The premise is the same. You might not have ever been grounded fully in your body or connected to the Earth, but as you tap into *their* grounding cord, you experience what it is like to feel safe in your body. This is a peaceful, easy feeling that gives you more confidence and makes you feel secure. But one person is not meant to be a sustainable ground for another. There are people who don't mind it and are really good at grounding more than one person at a time, but truly, we all have our own connection with the Earth.

The problem with using another person for grounding is that eventually they will get tired or withdraw into their own world, and you will be lacking a pathway for grounding. The best source of grounding you can find is never in another person; it is re-membering your own connection to the planet.

Reconnecting to the Earth

If you think you might be grounding through another person, sense your grounding cord. Your grounding cord is located at your perineum between your genitals and your anus.

Is it going straight down into the Earth?

Does it feel strong and firm?

If not, take some time to sense where you are connected to another person. Loosen the connection and return it back to them. Then send your energy cord right into the center of the Earth. Feel yourself sinking down into your body. Relax and feel your Root Chakra opening and expanding as your grounding cord opens and expands. The more relaxed you are, the more open and deep your Root Chakra goes into the Earth. You are safe and you are loved.

How do you feel now?

Can you feel the difference in the connection?

What are your emotions?

How much more centered do you feel?

Here is another way of looking at it that goes to the core belief of why you are attracting this kind of relationship or attachment.

Built-In Keys to Freedom

Each chakra holds a key to freedom. Each placement of an energy cord will tell you exactly why you connect in the way that you do, and how you can create wholeness in the places that were filled with other people's energy. When we are lacking, or feel that we are lacking, we will try to fill those places with something outside ourselves, usually a partner. This works for a while, and we feel full and complete, hence the phrase, "You complete me." Sure, okay, your partner does complete you, but it's like a patch job. Think of it as an energetic fix-a-flat, that can of compressed air you put in your tire if you have a flat so that you can get to the nearest gas station, where your tire can be truly fixed.

Does it work?

Sure it does, but is the fix sustainable?

No. Eventually you will need to use another fix-a-flat can or you have to get the tire fixed.

Can someone constantly fill you up so that you feel full?

Sure, but eventually they will start to feel depleted, and you will start to feel yucky, because when you count on getting your energy from another person instead of the Earth or Divine Source, you will eventually run out. Humans are not a good source of energy. They become tired, are unreliable, and will eventually resent that you get all your energy from them. The truth is, you don't need to get it from them when you can simply tap into your own energy source.

Why do I mention this?

When you are holding on to someone else's energy because you are afraid to let them go, you are most likely doing this for one or more of the following reasons:

1. **You are afraid that if you let go of their energy you will never feel love like this again.**

   Do you really feel that love right now?

   Or are you feeling pain because you are *remembering* that you once did feel love, and now you are holding onto this pain and pretending you are feeling love?

And if you keep holding onto this energy, you will never find love again because there is no space for you to welcome another person's love.

2. **They gave me this energy so now it's mine.**
Is this true?

Does it feel like your energy?

If it were your energy, why would you say it was someone else's energy?

Someone else's energy is never going to be *your* energy. You can feel it, you can take it in and swish it around with your own energy, but it will never assimilate into your field because it is not yours. It's like getting a blood transfusion with the wrong kind of blood. Eventually it will stagnate and keep you from accessing your own energy and power.

3. **They need me to hold on to this for them. I am helping.**
No, you really aren't. No one can heal something that is not theirs. We all have lessons to learn in this lifetime, but we cannot learn someone else's lessons for them.

You may believe, "Oh, that poor person, let me take their burdens from them so they won't have to go through that anymore." But there is a reason they picked this lesson, whatever it is. They picked it so they could learn it and get to the other side, so if you take this away from them, they will usually recreate the challenge anyway until they understand whatever the lesson is. In the meantime, you have an energy in your field that is not serving you and you cannot heal it, because it's not yours to heal. When you return this energy back to the person it belongs to, they will feel a burst of energy, and they will know what to do with it. It's a gift all the way around. If you still don't want to give this energy back to them because you are afraid it will burden them, then give it to Divine Source. Divine Source will know how to help them better than you can.

The same goes for energy cords.

1. **I need to keep this cord attached because we are soul mates.** This is not a healthy life partner cord. This is a cord of fear. The connection you have with another person is eternal, and you don't need a cord for that. We establish these cords out of fear of losing the other person.

   Think of the energy cord as putting someone on a leash. You want to hold onto the leash so they will not go away, but the interesting part is that if you truly release the cord, you will probably feel closer to them. You will be able to see them clearly as a person instead of someone you need to hold on to for dear life. The cords warp your connection and cause more of a needy, clingy energy. If you are able to release the cord, you will feel more peaceful and so will they.
2. **If I let go of this cord, I will be alone.** Don't you feel alone right now?

   The lie we tell ourselves is that this cord keeps us tethered to another so we don't have to be alone, but it is actually doing the opposite. It is causing us to look to another person to feel complete and connected. Ultimately it will only make us feel sad and alone, because the connection you are looking for isn't actually with another person. It is with Source Energy. We sometimes misidentify human connection as Source connection. And then we get mad at the person because they are not giving us everything we need. In truth, it's not their job. It's our job to connect to Source energy to fulfill our needs.

   If your ex was constantly telling you they needed space, yet you hardly spent time together, chances are that they had too much of your energy in the energy field around their body. If you find yourself thinking about your ex constantly and obsessively, it is likely that you have their energy in the energy field around your body.

Having someone else's energy in your energy field can feel really good in the beginning. It's fun and energizing, but eventually what happens is that it slows down and stagnates, and you begin to feel gunky. When you look inside to figure out why you feel gunky, that person is the first person that comes to mind. The reason is not because they did anything wrong specifically, but because you have their energy floating around in your energetic space.

However, another person's old stagnant energy only feels gunky to you because it is not yours. Once you release it back to them they will feel a burst of pure energy, because it is energy that is resonant and perfect for *them*. The same goes for you. Once you call your energy back from wherever you left it, you will feel a surge of energy because you will be getting back energy that is specifically for you.

Reclaiming Your Energy

Take a moment to get your body and mind into a relaxed state. Tune into your body and identify where you feel heavy or gunky. Ask to whom this foreign energy belongs. You will get an idea, and if you don't, don't worry about it. You can still send the energy back to them.

Focus on the foreign energy, take a deep breath, and breathe it out through your mouth with the intention of breathing it back to whomever it belongs to. Keep breathing and focusing until your body feels clear and you don't have any more thoughts of the person in question.

Now start breathing in through your nose with the intention that all the energy you have given comes back to you cleansed and purified. As you breathe in, imagine pulling all your energy back into your body, into your head and down into your body, filling you up. Keep breathing like this until you feel complete.

CHAPTER 9

Emotions—Why They Come Up and How to Clear Them

Sadness, Grieving, and Loneliness

Many times when you get together with a partner, you are filled with vitality, joy, and hope for life and the future. The colors in nature seem so much brighter, and everything feels like it belongs in a fairy tale, a beautiful new adventure. Miracles happen in every moment, and you feel you are divinely blessed.

When your relationship starts to break down, it seems that everything begins to fall apart and nothing is as it should be. Colors look gray and life is not as fun as it used to be. But why?

How could someone else affect your life so much and in such a profound way?

I believe that everyone on this planet is looking for a connection to the Source. You could call it the Divine, the Universe, or God, but basically it is that feeling of being totally safe, unconditionally loved, and fully resonant to the highest energy you can imagine. You feel free to be yourself and open to new possibilities.

When we fall in love with someone, we give ourselves a free pass to feel this way, to feel connected, open and free. In doing this I believe that we begin to believe that this person *is* our Source Energy. They become our Source for happiness, love and Divine connection. The problem with this is that one human does not have enough energy to sustain another human for extended periods of time. Your partner might be able to give you the love and energy you are looking for, for a while, but eventually they will come up short on energy and will not be able to give you what you need. This does not mean there is something wrong with you or with them, it just means they are human, and as a human they are not built to be a battery for you. That is an important thing to reiterate. Do not depend on humans for your energy needs. They will fail you every time—it may not happen right away, but it will happen eventually.

As infinite beings, we do not need energy because we *are* energy. We have access to everything we need at all times, but our physical body does need energy. Without it we cannot function. Our physical body is fueled by our energetic presence. When we are not focused on our body or our focus is somewhere else with someone else, our body will become low on energy and it will begin to look for ways to fill itself back up again. Here are some ways it may try to get a quick fix.

Humans

When we have interactions with others, we exchange energy with them. Sometimes it is reciprocal. Sometimes one person needs more energy than the other, and one person might feel drained from the interaction. Other times, the interaction can inspire and raise the vibration of both people. The problem with getting energy from other people is that it is finite. Exchanging energy with people is fun and helps in the moment, but it is not a sustainable way to vitalize yourself on a consistent basis.

Pets

Pets, like humans, will give us a quick fix of energy with their unconditional love. Their job in our lives is to remind us of unconditional love. When we feel unconditional love, our energy field opens up, and we allow our energetic body to fully merge with our physical body. But pets, just like humans, are not designed to be full-time energy sources for humans, so it is important not to depend on them for all your energy needs.

Food

We eat food to nourish our cells. Our body metabolizes the food and gives us energy, but food also releases life force energy as we eat it. The more fresh and raw food is, the more energy it will give us. The tricky part of this balance is that if your body is not getting the specific nutrients it needs, it will tend to give you a signal to continue eating. The more raw food we eat, the less we will need to consume because the more nutrients there will be. When people eat foods with fewer nutrients, the body will ask us to continue eating because it is not getting all that it needs. It figures that if you eat enough food, it will eventually get what it needs, but this only creates a feeling of insatiability that makes us unhappy and never satisfied.

This brings up another good point: if we are not getting the correct nutrients in our diet, or if we are eating foods that we are allergic to, it can cause us to fall into depression.

When going through a breakup, there is a tendency to want to eat comfort foods, which are usually dairy and sugar-based. These will give us a feeling of sedation, but will not bring us sustained joy. Better choices might be root vegetables because they help you to feel more grounded in your body. Roasted beets, carrots, and sweet potatoes are all helpful in creating a feeling of comfort while helping the body to feel relaxed and grounded.

If you are sad, the best thing you can do for your body is to give it light and nutritious foods so that it can feel lighter during heavy times.

Music

Tones and musical vibrations can uplift you in a moment. Create a playlist of uplifting music you can turn to when you feel sad. Singing songs or creating different tones with your voice can help to shift stagnant, heavy energy out of your energy field. Singing and music help you to shift because of the frequencies in the music. When you are sad, the energy in your body is usually vibrating at a very low frequency. Musical tones can help it to shift frequency simply by playing them.

I use toning as a way to sense energy that is low or stuck in my body. I will voice certain tones and focus on different parts of my body. As I do, a certain tone will come out and the more I tone and focus on a specific area, the more it begins to shift. The tone will usually go from a low note to a higher note and then stay at the higher frequency. That is how I know I am complete in a specific area. This can be done for physical pains in the body as well as emotions.

I also tone through the chakras. There are certain sounds that are specific to each chakra, which you can research if you like. Or you can simply trust that your body will create the correct sound for you while you try out different toning sounds.

Nature

Going out into nature, breathing in fresh air, feeling your bare feet on the earth, or lying on the ground will help super-charge you with sustainable energy from plants, trees, the Earth, and the sun. Scientific studies show that when you walk barefoot or lay on the ground for forty minutes or more it will actually shift your blood chemistry. Read more about Earthing or grounding on Clint Ober's website: www.groundology.com. He wrote the book on this subject, *Earthing: The Most Important Health Discovery Ever?*

Clearing Meditation/Healing Meditation

Do you ever take on other people's energy?

Do they tell you their problems, and then afterwards you feel as if you are coated in yucky goo, or are very tired?

People who are sensitive to the feelings or emotions of others are sometimes called *empaths*. Empaths tend to take on the feelings, thoughts, and emotions of others, and most of the time they are not aware of how to release or let go of this energy. In the next section I have included an exercise to help you to release the energy of others, which could be keeping sadness cycling for you. Sometimes we take on sadness from other people, and if that happens we can try to heal it and shift it. But you cannot heal what is not yours. The only way to clear this energy is to give it back to whomever you took it on from. I have developed a special, gentle, and compassionate technique for this so that as you release the energy, you also send with it a guide that will teach that person what to do with the energy once it returns to them.

Many times we think we are helping others by taking away their lesson or their pain, but in actuality they asked for this lesson for a reason. If you take it away, they will create another opportunity for it to come up, and then you end up with some heavy feelings you did not create. It's like smearing yourself with someone else's poo . . . it doesn't help them, it doesn't help you, plus nobody wants to be around you, because you stink!

When you release someone's energy back to them, they get to learn the lesson they were intending to learn and are freed from having to recreate it again. And just so you know, the person you release the energy back to doesn't experience it as poo, or anything bad, they just get an influx of their own energy.

When you connect to Divine Source or Universal Source Energy, it can be used indefinitely. It is an unlimited amount of energy you can tap into. Most people have forgotten or never learned how to tap into it, so I have included the following exercise to help you with clearing.

Clearing Sadness

Find a comfortable place to rest. You want to be fully and completely relaxed to allow these suggestions flow through you and create the changes you wish to receive.

Now, take a deep breath, and let's begin.

Focusing on the top of your head and all the muscles in and around the top of your head. As you breathe into these muscles, allow them to release, relax, and let go.

Focusing on your face, breathe and relax into your face, allowing all the muscles in and around your face to deeply relax with each and every breath.

Moving to the back of your head now, breathe and relax all of the muscles in and around the back of your head. Allowing each and every breath to bring you deeper into relaxation.

Allowing this relaxation to move down into your neck and shoulders. Breathing into your neck and shoulders, feeling so good so relaxed as you take another deep breath, allowing these muscles to release, relax and let go.

Feeling this relaxation move down into your arms and hands as you continue to relax and breathe. Letting go of all stress and tension as you take another deep breath.

As you breathe even more deeply, notice the rise and fall of your chest with each and every inhale and exhale. Notice how much more relaxed you are becoming. Each and every breath bringing you deeper into relaxation.

Feel this relaxation moving into your back now as you breathe even more deeply, even more slowly. You are safe and you are loved. You are deeply supported in this and all moments. Continuing to relax and breathe.

Breathing down into your belly, relaxing into your belly. Allow it to open and soften with each and every breath.

Breathe down into your hips and all the muscles in and around your hips. Feeling so good, so relaxed.

Moving down into your bottom, allowing all these muscles to release, relax, and let go.

Moving your awareness down into your thighs, and all the muscles in and around your thighs, releasing, relaxing, and letting go. Feel the relaxation moving down into your knees, and all the muscles in and around your knees, as you continue down into your shins and calves. Allow your shins, and calves to release, relax, and let go.

Moving down into your ankles, breathing into your ankles, allow them to release, relax, and let go.

Take another deep breath and moving down into your feet and toes. Allow the relaxation to ow into all the muscles in your feet and toes, and let your toes know that it's okay to relax.

Scan your body to sense the location of the sadness you are experiencing.

Is it in a specific place in your body?

Is it all over your body?

I know it might feel intense, but take some time to breathe into this feeling. Go right into the center of it. The only way to release this feeling is to feel it, so know that you are safe and you are loved and everything is going to be okay. This feeling is not you, you are simply experiencing a sensation. When you get caught up in a TV show or a movie, you may feel emotional, but those feeling are only your reactions to a story. These feelings cannot truly harm the part of you that is eternal.

As you feel deeply into this place, ask yourself: "Does this feeling belong to me or someone else?"

If it feels as if the answer is no, move deeper into this feeling. Take a deep breath and, with your intention, breathe it back to whomever it belongs, with the instructions that when they receive this energy they will know exactly what to do with it. You can also call in a spiritual guide to travel with the energy and make sure that it is received and to help the person to transmute it and heal.

The feeling might intensify, but just continue to relax, breathe, and open up.

Continue to breathe and release this energy until it subsides.

If you feel as though the energy does belong to you, feel into it and ask the energy what it wants you to know. Many times this energy is a younger aspect of yourself who needs a bit of healing.

Ask this part of yourself, "How old are you?"

"Why are you sad?"

"What would make you feel better?"

Talk to this part of yourself just as you would a small child. Love and nurture this younger self. Keep breathing and relaxing into this energy. The more relaxed you are, the easier it is for them to release. Know that you are safe and you are loved, and let this younger part of yourself know this, too.

As you acknowledge this energy, it should begin to dissipate. This part of you just wants to feel safe and loved, so during this time it's your job to re-parent your younger self. Give this aspect all the love it needs. Tell your younger self all the things you have been waiting for a partner or a parent to tell you. As you start to fill this younger you with love and affection, you will feel the sadness and loneliness ease.

Continue this process until you feel whole, peaceful, and complete.

Imagine now a white-golden light filling up the space around you. This light clears away all that is not you and attracts only the highest vibrations of love and light.

As you breathe, this light penetrates every cell of your body. Light surrounds you, penetrates you, and fills you with a peaceful, loving feeling. You are light; you are love; you are infinite; you are so much more than enough.

Take a deep breath and take in this feeling, the feeling of your true self. You are a beautiful physical being of pure light. Allow this light to expand around you and within you. You are safe and you are loved. You are complete and you are free.

Bring this light fully and completely into your body and allow it to flow into your feet. Feel the energy flowing from the top of your head down your body and into your feet. Feel yourself filling back into your body and occupying every cell.

Really own this physical body. Make it yours. Come back in until you feel completely full and completely at home.

Anger

During a breakup you may feel rage or anger surfacing. For some, these emotions help to push through a difficult time. If we are feeling anger it lends us a bit of passion and fire to get things done, to burn a path through blockages. Metabolizing sadness or heavy energy with the fire of anger or rage can be very cathartic. You can run the feelings of anger and rage through your body without directing it at anyone. That is the safest way to process it.

The way to do this is to come into a relaxed, meditative place (this can be challenging when you are upset, but try your best).

Tune into the feelings of the anger and rage in your body. Feel them flowing through your body, coursing through your veins. Now bring your awareness back behind the anger; simply observe it. Open up a space for it to flow through your body. Be aware that this is not you. These are chemicals running through your body; these are feelings you are experiencing, but they are not you. Just sit in a peaceful place as you feel them and observe them, but do not identify with them. The anger will eventually subside. All fires eventually burn out, and your feelings are no exception to this natural law.

Most of the time, anger signifies a boundary violation, or it can be a tool that allows us to reach a better feeling than sadness or depression. There is a spiritual consciousness teacher called Abraham, translated by Esther Hicks, who talks about an emotional scale (abraham-hicks.com). The higher you are on the emotional scale, the higher your energy vibration and the happier you are. When you are blissfully happy, you are said to be *in the Vortex*. The Vortex is a vibrational place where everything you have ever wanted is present. When you are happy, positive, and in an emotionally high vibration state, you are better able to attract into your life what it is that you truly want. Many people think that the things they want are being withheld from them, but what this school of thought says is that if you get happy and raise your vibration high enough, everything you have ever wanted will be found in the Vortex, waiting for you.

It's not always easy to get into the Vortex. You can't always go from feeling depressed to feeling blissful, but you can make your way up the feeling scale. Grief and depression are at the very end of the list, while anger is a little higher on the list. If you are sad or depressed, then anger is what you experience when heavy energy begins to move, so it is helping you make your way up the scale. This is not to suggest you should stay in anger, but it will help you to make your way to better and better feeling emotions.

This is not a complete list, and you may be able to leap over some emotions to access higher vibrations.

Emotional Scale

1. Joy/appreciation/empowerment/freedom/love
2. Passion
3. Enthusiasm/eagerness/happiness
4. Positive expectation/belief
5. Optimism
6. Hopefulness
7. Contentment
8. Boredom
9. Pessimism
10. Frustration/irritation/impatience
11. Overwhelmed
12. Disappointment

13. Doubt
14. Worry
15. Blame
16. Discouragement
17. Anger
18. Revenge
19. Hatred/rage
20. Jealousy
21. Insecurity/guilt/unworthiness
22. Fear/grief/depression/despair/powerlessness

Anxiety and Abandonment

Anxiety and abandonment are the result of giving away our power to another person. We have given this person the authority over us to make us happy or sad. We looked to this person to fulfill us or to make us whole. Many times we will feel a tug in our solar plexus or stomach area. This is our power center, the place where our will originates. When the person to whom we have connected leaves us, we can experience a sense of powerlessness or complete failure. When we realign this chakra, our power comes back to us and we feel content and strong again.

The reason we give away our power to others often stems from our need to feel loved and accepted. If we did not feel loved and accepted as a child, we will often look to others to love and accept us in life, and this often shows up in the partners we choose. The way to heal this issue is to love and accept ourselves fully and completely.

Explore those thoughts of anxiety and abandonment and ask them how old they are. Ask them what they want. And then imagine giving them what they need. Again, it is about re-parenting these parts of yourself, giving yourself the love and safety you never got as a child.

Re-parenting yourself is the most sustainable way to give yourself the love you require. It will create a permanent feeling of love and safety because it comes from you. *You* are the person you have been waiting for. You might think you have been waiting for someone else to come into your life and love you completely, but in truth **the words and the voice that will make the biggest impact on you *are your own*.**

During our lifetime, our internal self-talk can be rough. What we say to ourselves daily can be worse than what any enemy would say. We can tear ourselves down deeply and be our own worst critic. When we begin the journey of re-parenting ourselves, it might take a bit of time for trust to be established. You might not feel safe at first, but stay with it and give it time. It's like getting to know a new friend or lover. Be patient, gentle, and loving, and if you find yourself falling back into old patterns, apologize and begin again.

Unworthiness

If a partner leaves you, energetically and emotionally you may feel a sense of lack or unworthiness, as if you do not deserve happiness anymore. You may feel that if this person does not love you, then no one will. There is an energetic shift that happens when someone leaves us, either through a breakup or through death or distance.

We feel a lack in who we are and our connection to everyone and everything, mostly because we have given our power away to this other person. This means that we have made this other person more important than ourselves. We have decided on some level that their opinion of us is more important than our own. However, this does not mean we are at a loss forever. We can shift back into our own power and self-love again.

One of the reasons we feel a lack of love is because our source of love was this other person. When we focus more on another person for love rather than giving ourselves the love we need from ourselves, we can feel lonely. The loneliness is not there because the other person doesn't love us. It exists because we have more energy invested in another and very little in our own body. The loneliness we are experiencing is our body's loneliness for our own love and energy. As we begin to take the focus off the other person and start focusing on ourselves again, that sense of love and fulfillment returns to us. Instead of looking to another for our love, validation, and completion, we can focus our attention on our own body and our connection to Divine Love.

To Clear Feelings of Unworthiness

Find a comfortable place to rest. You want to be fully and completely relaxed to allow these suggestions flow through you and create the changes you wish to receive.

Now, take a deep breath, and let's begin.

Focusing on the top of your head and all the muscles in and around the top of your head. As you breathe into these muscles, allow them to release, relax, and let go.

Focusing on your face, breathe and relax into your face, allowing all the muscles in and around your face to deeply relax with each and every breath.

Moving to the back of your head now, breathe and relax all of the muscles in and around the back of your head. Allowing each and every breath to bring you deeper into relaxation.

Allowing this relaxation to move down into your neck and shoulders. Breathing into your neck and shoulders, feeling so good so relaxed as you take another deep breath, allowing these muscles to release, relax and let go.

Feeling this relaxation move down into your arms and hands as you continue to relax and breathe. Letting go of all stress and tension as you take another deep breath.

As you breathe even more deeply, notice the rise and fall of your chest with each and every inhale and exhale. Notice how much more relaxed you are becoming. Each and every breath bringing you deeper into relaxation.

Feel this relaxation moving into your back now as you breathe even more deeply, even more slowly. You are safe and you are loved. You are deeply supported in this and all moments. Continuing to relax and breathe.

Breathing down into your belly, relaxing into your belly. Allow it to open and soften with each and every breath.

Breathe down into your hips and all the muscles in and around your hips. Feeling so good, so relaxed.

Moving down into your bottom, allowing all these muscles to release, relax, and let go.

Moving your awareness down into your thighs, and all the muscles in and around your thighs, releasing, relaxing, and letting go. Feel the relaxation moving down into your knees, and all the muscles in and around your knees, as you continue down into your shins and calves. Allow your shins, and calves to release, relax, and let go.

Moving down into your ankles, breathing into your ankles, allow them to release, relax, and let go.

Take another deep breath and moving down into your feet and toes. Allow the relaxation to ow into all the muscles in your feet and toes, and let your toes know that it's okay to relax.

Put your hands on your chest and breathe deeply. Tune into this area. Feel the rise and fall of your chest as you breathe in and out.

How does this feel?

Tune into these feelings. Breathe into them. Many times people have a tendency to move away from feelings of pain or discomfort, but for now, let's move into them and see what happens. You are safe and loved, and it's okay to feel your feelings. Take a deep breath and move deeper into the sensation.

How does it feel?

Is it a tightening or an ache?

Does it have a color, a sound, or a taste?

Any way it is showing up for you is okay; simply stay with it and explore all its aspects. Notice what happens when you breathe fully into this place. Don't get caught up in any story about the feeling, just observe. Settle more into the feeling with your intention. Imagine sitting in the middle of the sensation and breathing, expanding it with your breath. You are safe and you are loved. Keep breathing and focusing your attention here.

Now imagine a white light emanating from you in the center of this place.

How does this space feel now?

Is there any change in the sensation?

Intensify the brightness. If you can't see the color or the light, just imagine it or feel it happening. We are just experimenting, so you can't get this wrong. Everything that we do here is exploration and experiment.

If the sensations in this place could talk to you, what would they say? What are they trying to tell you? How old is the person who is expressing these feelings? Many times this is a younger aspect of us who is hurt and has never recovered from an event that happened a long time ago. Sit with this part of you and hold space for it . . . allow it to be seen and heard . . . hold it in a loving embrace. Be the parent that this younger aspect of you needs. Be the strong shoulder they can count on. You are older now; you have the ability to give this part of you the love that it longs for.

Ask yourself:

Where did these feelings of unworthiness come from?

Did they ever truly belong to me?

Did I acquire them from someone else?

As babies, we come into this world loving ourselves, but as we grow we begin to take on the thoughts, feelings, and emotions of others. If you are not feeling pure love, you have probably taken on this feeling from someone else. Tune into it and breathe it back to the person you took it on from. We can only heal what is ours. If this energy has been with you for a long time, and you have not been able to shift it, chances are that it's not yours, so release it from you now. With awareness, send it back to the person it came from so they can heal as only they know how.

Please be aware that it only feels yucky to you because it is not your energy. When they get it back it will just feel like an infusion of energy to them. This is a gift for you both: you get to be free and they get

a piece of themselves back. You don't have to know to whom it is going or where it came from; simply form the intention that it goes where it needs to go. Keep breathing the energy out until you feel clear and free.

Now with your intention breathe in all the energy you have given out to others and bring it back to you. Just as this energy was feeling heavy to you in your body, this energy is probably feeling heavy in their body, too, so with your intention breathe it back into your body now. I like to imagine it flying in through the universe back to me as I inhale through my nose. Then I feel it settling into my body, filling me up with my own energy, cleansed and purified as it comes into my energetic field. Continue breathing your energy back until you feel full and complete. Right now, in this moment, let this part of you know how proud you are, how beautiful and smart they are. Let her know that you unconditionally love them, simply for being. Remind them that they are safe and loved. Repeat this gently as many times as needed.

Breathe deeply into this place. Allow them to relax and let go. Let them know that you are going to take care of them from now on. They don't have to worry anymore, you are here now and everything is going to be okay. Imagine hugging this part of yourself. Wrap your arms around this beautiful small child that is you. Again, if you can't see them, just make the intention that she receive this loving energy. Create this feeling in your own body.

Now that you are clear, let's take a trip together. Hold my hand and let's go back to the time before time. Relax and allow your consciousness to bring you back. Take a deep breath and relax. You are safe and you are loved.

Imagine now that we are standing in a beautiful place filled with light, a place where we are pure consciousness. Tune into how it feels to be here, and with each and every breath expand into this feeling of light consciousness. You are inhaling light. You are exhaling light. You are light.

See or feel your body expanding and contracting as you inhale and exhale this pure brilliant light. The light runs through you, encompasses you. You are pure Divine light and you emanate love. In this place, you are infinite. You always were and you always will be. You are a part of consciousness and you are consciousness itself. Breathe in this feeling of expansive freedom.

There was a flash, an instant when you decided you would like to experience limitation. Just to see what it would be like, instead of feeling everything at once, you would limit your experience and incarnate in a body. In order to create this limitation you had to pick some things you wanted to learn about—love, worthiness, power—you picked different lessons to learn and programed your energy field to attract these things into your life.

You chose parents, a body, and friends who would help you fulfill these goals, and you incarnated on to the planet in physical form. When you got here, the way that everyone helped you to experience these things wasn't always easy.

Sometimes it felt like you were alone and abandoned by the ones you loved, but your infinite self knows this is all part of the process of learning. Everything that is happening here is to help you learn something more, to help you learn how to return to love.

Take a moment now to remember a difficult time in your life. Relive the feelings of sadness, loss, and devastation.

Now call in your infinite self, that part of you that knows who you are. Ask this part of yourself to love and surround this painful moment. Allow yourself to experience all the pain in great detail, in all of its intensity. Surrender into it. Feel it all. And now let this grace of the infinite consciousness infuse and surround it in light. Breathe the light into it. Allow this light to merge with the feelings. Allow this light to transform them into pure energy consciousness. Feel and experience the feelings, because that is why we are here, to feel them and experience them, then allow them to be transformed.

There is a mechanism that makes us want to hold on to the feelings. This is because we are programmed to want to learn the lesson. But what if feeling the feelings is the lesson, and if we feel it we can then allow it to be transformed. Know that as you dive into these feelings, they will not consume you. You will not get lost in them. They will not last forever. You are safe and you are loved. You are never alone during this process: we are with you.

Take a deep breath. Go into these feelings and breathe deeply. Allow yourself to feel it all. Allow the tears to flow or the confusion to arise. Anything you feel is okay, simply allow it all to come and feel it all. Now call in your

infinite light consciousness. Allow it to merge with you and encompass you, infusing into each and every cell of your being. This is you. Remember who you are as an infinite being.

You are light.

You are love.

You are this light and energy, and you are this body.

You are everything and nothing.

Continue breathing in light and breathing out light. You are this light. Remember who you are as this infinite being. You are Divine love. You are light and you are free. Remember this feeling, and remember who you truly are. You can do anything because you are everything. You are light, you are love, and you are free.

Take the time now to come back into your body. Focus now on breathing yourself back into this physical body of yours. Allow the light and energy to hold a permanent place within your physical body, allowing you to feel lighter and freer, yet being more present in your physical body. Allow yourself to settle all the way into your physical body. Fill in all the places that have been vacant. Fill them up with you. This is your body, your soul's mate, so settle in, with love.

Feel yourself becoming more present here. You are safe and you are loved. You are whole, you are complete, and you belong here.

CHAPTER 10

Soul Mates and Twin Flames

The original soul mate story was presented in Plato's *The Symposium*, in which Aristophanes states that humans originally had four arms, four legs, and a single head made of two faces. Men were children of the Sun and women were children of the Earth.

The Gods were afraid that these beings were going to become more powerful than they were, so they thought to destroy them with lightning, but then Zeus had another idea. He decided that they could split these beings in half, distracting them and keeping them forever searching for their other half. When they finally found their other half, they would feel a joy unbounded and a sense of completion in one another.

I guess that could be a good explanation as to why we meet some people and feel like we have known them forever and feel a sense of completion with them. It seems easy and effortless to speak to them, and we have an instant energy connection and familiarity that we just cannot explain.

However, there are many problems with this theory. Many people I have talked to, including myself, are having many of these kinds of interactions in this lifetime. In the original theory there is only one, so how can we meet more than one?

One idea is that we have a soul family, that is, many people we came here to interact with and have relationships with during this lifetime. When we meet these people, we feel a natural affinity for them, but we are not necessarily supposed to ride off into the sunset with them or marry them. Perhaps they have some lessons for us or we have one for them. Perhaps we have a project to complete with one another.

If we decide that these feelings mean that we are supposed to be in a romantic relationship and yet it doesn't work out that way, we feel devastated because we think we have lost our one chance at being eternally happy. This can be a sad, messed-up story to tell ourselves. Do we really believe that if one person doesn't work out, we are doomed to live out the rest of our days sad and alone?

No thanks. I am not buying this, and you don't have to either.

Another theory about soul mates is based on vibrations. When I am in a happy, high vibration, when I am feeling a sense of total and complete love within myself, I attract lovers into my life that are an amazing match for me and everything I have been asking for. (I talk more about how to achieve this in the next section, "Divine Lover.") Basically, as we become a full and complete person and lover, we rise up in vibration, and when we hit a certain frequency, the person we have been wanting and praying for meets us there. Or, more appropriately, we are there to meet them. Everyone that we have ever wanted is waiting for us to rise to meet them. It seems like a catch-22 because you would be so happy if you were with them, but in order to have them come into your life, you need to be happy and of a high vibration. And once you are that happy in your own being, you won't even need them anymore, instead, they will simply be a fun bonus to your complete life.

An interesting side note to this is that when we are in a high vibration, we feel complete with one another. However, as our vibration lowers and we are feeling less whole and complete within ourselves, feeling small and needy, our relationships with everyone tend to break down. We start to see faults in others, and they see faults within us.

The reason for this is because we are meant to meet everyone on a higher frequency. That is our natural state of being. When we leave that frequency, the aspects of them we had been interacting with are no longer present because we are not present in that same frequency anymore. Another way of looking at this is to imagine listening to jazz music, but then turning the radio dial to a country station. It's not wrong or bad; we simply won't find what we are looking for at that station. We need to turn the dial back to the frequency we want to experience. If we want to experience a feeling of Divine Love, we must be on a frequency of Divine Love.

Another view is that no matter who shows up in our lives, they will match the frequency that we are emanating. The fault is never with another for the way things are showing up in our lives: it's up to us to shift our vibration.

Divine Lover

During the process of seeking my soul mate, I discovered something that I call my Divine Lover. Between you and Source Energy (you can call it God, Infinite Energy, or imagine it as the highest energy you can think of), there is a meeting of minds. The Divine Lover is a translator of Divine Energy into human speech. It's basically the personality version of God. Some call it the I AM presence or identify it as a guardian angel.

This energy is you, but also understands things from a more expansive level. Oftentimes we are living life on a personality level and we become lost or confused. The Divine part of us is never confused because it is always connected to Source energy. As we talk to this part of ourselves, we can get the answers we are looking for because it knows us completely, and it is connected to Source, so it's a win-win. It's our very own personalized spiritual Google.

For me, however, it's more than a source of knowledge: it's also my very best friend. This part of me presents itself as male energy, and it's everything I could ever want in a male counterpart. It knows what makes me laugh and knows what needs to be said to me in exactly the way I need to hear it, because it is me.

This may seem a bit schizophrenic, but truly, everyone has access to this presence. It's that voice that tells you everything is going to be okay when you are feeling low. It's that part of you that tells you the answer when you really don't know. When an answer comes "out of nowhere," it's usually coming from the Divine Lover.

When I am feeling lonely or am missing having a partner in my life, this is the energy I call upon to fill me up. I ask him to come and talk to me or wrap his arms around me when I sleep. This energy is everything you have been looking for in a partner except for the intimate physical contact.

Here is where it gets interesting: When you communicate with this essence of yourself and really get to know it and love it, something amazing happens. You will begin to vibrate at a frequency of already having a beautiful perfect partner in your life, and when you are vibrating at that frequency, you attract just that. You actually magnetize to you the person in physical form that most closely resembles this relationship you have with your Divine Lover.

I guess you could say that it is like having a practice partner, but you can even keep this relationship going when you have a physical partner. In fact, it is good to keep this relationship throughout your whole lifetime, as it will make you less needy or clingy to a physical partner, because all your emotional needs will be fulfilled on a daily basis. You will be able to interact with your partner on a physical, home-loving, playful level, and not as someone you need to fulfill your purpose in life.

How To Contact Your Divine Lover

Find a comfortable place to rest. You want to be fully and completely relaxed to allow these suggestions flow through you and create the changes you wish to receive.

Now, take a deep breath, and let's begin.

Focusing on the top of your head and all the muscles in and around the top of your head. As you breathe into these muscles, allow them to release, relax, and let go.

Focusing on your face, breathe and relax into your face, allowing all the muscles in and around your face to deeply relax with each and every breath.

Moving to the back of your head now, breathe and relax all of the muscles in and around the back of your head. Allowing each and every breath to bring you deeper into relaxation.

Allowing this relaxation to move down into your neck and shoulders. Breathing into your neck and shoulders, feeling so good so relaxed as you take another deep breath, allowing these muscles to release, relax and let go.

Feeling this relaxation move down into your arms and hands as you continue to relax and breathe. Letting go of all stress and tension as you take another deep breath.

As you breathe even more deeply, notice the rise and fall of your chest with each and every inhale and exhale. Notice how much more relaxed you are becoming. Each and every breath bringing you deeper into relaxation.

Feel this relaxation moving into your back now as you breathe even more deeply, even more slowly. You are safe and you are loved. You are deeply supported in this and all moments. Continuing to relax and breathe.

Breathing down into your belly, relaxing into your belly. Allow it to open and soften with each and every breath.

Breathe down into your hips and all the muscles in and around your hips. Feeling so good, so relaxed.

Moving down into your bottom, allowing all these muscles to release, relax, and let go.

Moving your awareness down into your thighs, and all the muscles in and around your thighs, releasing, relaxing, and letting go.

Feel the relaxation moving down into your knees, and all the muscles in and around your knees, as you continue down into your shins and calves. Allow your shins, and calves to release, relax, and let go.

Moving down into your ankles, breathing into your ankles, allow them to release, relax, and let go.

Take another deep breath and moving down into your feet and toes. Allow the relaxation to flow into all the muscles in your feet and toes, and let your toes know that it's okay to relax.

Now imagine there is a cord of energy attached to the top of your head, and as you follow this cord of energy up, you encounter a beautiful glowing orb of white golden light. Within this orb, you find a person of the gender that you attracted to. If you have more masculine energy it will appear more feminine. If you are more feminine in nature, it will appear as more masculine.

Tune into this presence and feel the Divine Lover energy.

Does the Divine Lover feel familiar to you?

Take the time to talk to this Divine being.

What does this presence want you to know?

How can you contact this presence when you want to talk?

You can ask this Divine being anything you want to; nothing is off limits. This is you, only an amplified, super conscious you, so feel free to say and ask anything you would like to know.

Imagine now a white-golden light filling up the space around you. This light clears away all that is not you and attracts only the highest vibrations of love and light.

As you breathe, this light penetrates every cell of your body. Light surrounds you, penetrates you, and fills you with a peaceful, loving feeling. You are light; you are love; you are infinite; you are so much more than enough.

Take a deep breath and take in this feeling, the feeling of your true self. You are a beautiful physical being of pure light. Allow this light to expand around you and within you. You are safe and you are loved. You are complete and you are free.

Bring this light fully and completely into your body and allow it to flow into your feet. Feel the energy flowing from the top of your head down your body and into your feet. Feel yourself filling back into your body and occupying every cell.

Really own this physical body. Make it yours. Come back in until you feel completely full and completely at home.

CHAPTER 11

What Are Chakras?

Chakras are whirling vortexes of energy in the body that help us to process emotions as well as other energies around us. They help us understand psychological concepts such as survival, connection with others, assertion of our will, creation, love, acceptance, communication, gathering insights, and our connection to the Divine.

There are many chakras in the body; however, to keep things easy we will be focusing on the main seven. Don't worry if you don't know anything about chakras yet. I will be explaining each chakra in depth as we go through this process.

Why are we learning about chakras?

During the process of learning to *Move On and Let Go*, I realized that more was in play than only my heart when it came to relationships. Many patterns are set up throughout our lifetime that shape the way we interact with others. We may be having trouble communicating or connecting in a sexual way. Perhaps there are power plays involved in why a relationship did not work out. When we explore each chakra with the intention of clearing it, we get a deeper, more complete healing than would occur with cutting a simple energy cord. This type of clearing will reset your unhealthy energy patterns so you can attract a new partner without reliving the same stories again and again. If you have had a string of unhealthy relationships that seem as though they were all with the same person in different bodies, then you know what I am talking about. This process will allow you to figure out the pattern that is keeping you in the unhealthy loop and how to release it.

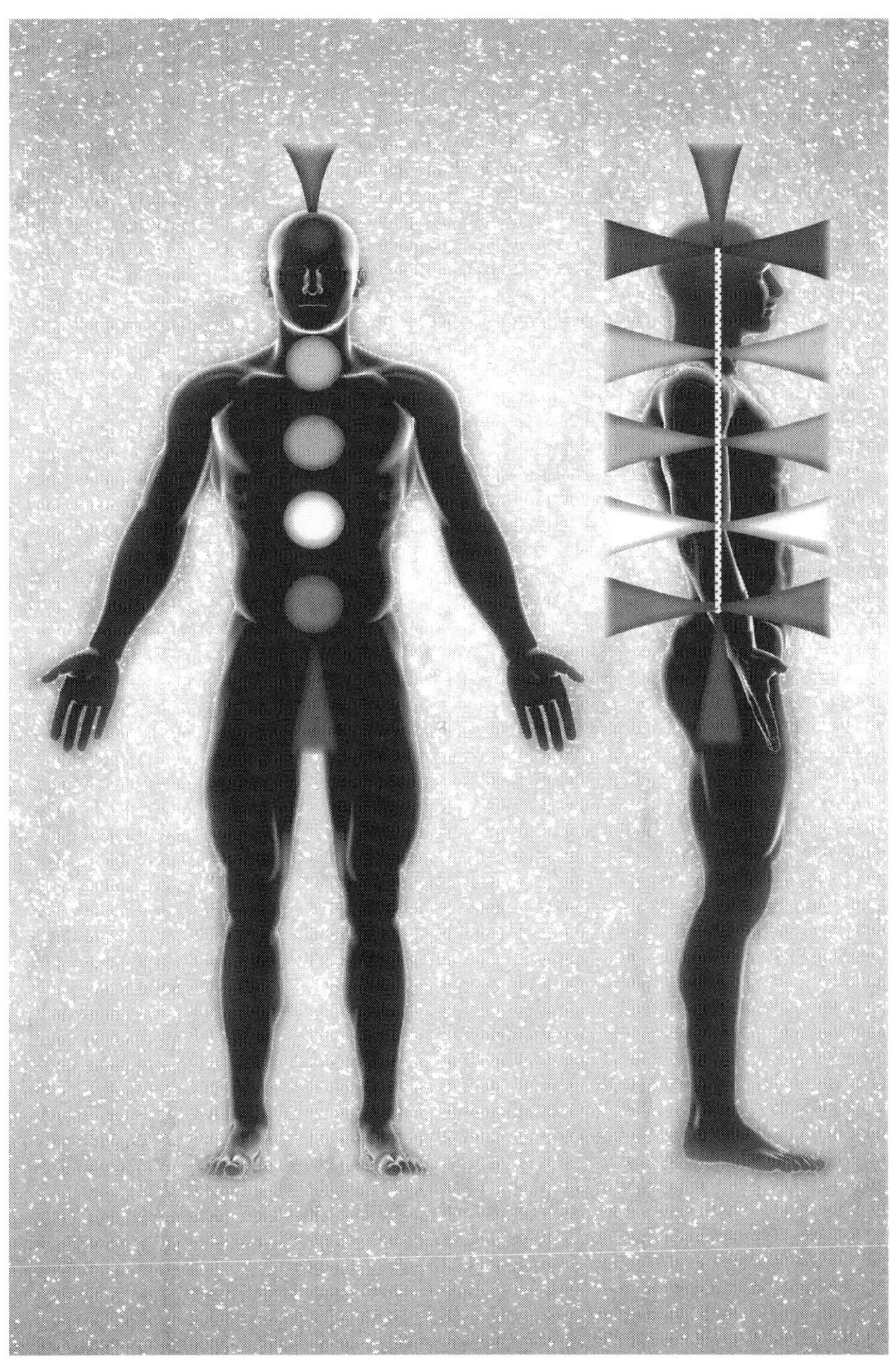

A Little More About How Chakras Work

When the chakras are open and clear, we feel a sense of peace, calm, and understanding about our place in the world. But when one of them is blocked, we begin to have trouble in the specific system that governs those issues. Let's say you have been having trouble with feeling safe. You feel afraid all the time and you never quite feel at home, even if you have been living in the same place for a long time. Chances are there is a blockage in your Root Chakra, the chakra that helps you to connect with the energies of being rooted in your body, to the earth and feeling at home wherever you are. Once you are able to clear, align, balance, and strengthen this chakra, the feelings of fear will be released and *even though your outside situation may be the same*, you will feel at peace.

An interesting side note: when your inner world changes, your outer world will eventually change with it. This is because as you shift your inner world, your vibration shifts and becomes more resonant with what it is that you want to attract into your life. When you are resonant with your true self—your happy, loving, connected self—then all the things and people you have desired to come into your life will start filtering in because they will be attracted to that same frequency, that same vibration you are resonating.

Recall that each chakra has a front and rear aspect, and they meet in the center of the body. All the front and rear chakras are connected together in a line of energy that goes from the top of the head down through the head and torso and out through the perineum. Chapters 12 through 18 will teach you how to clear, balance, align, and strengthen the front and rear chakras, as well as the connections, from the root chakra to the crown chakra. When all the chakras and connections are clear, you will feel strong, relaxed, integrated, and complete.

Chapter 12

Finding Your Grounding

Root Chakra

When you are in the process of letting someone go from your life, it may seem as though your whole foundation is crumbling, and in fact, it is. You come together with another person, and you become part of a collaborative life experience. You merge your thoughts, consciousness, and energy with your partner. You begin to see the world through each other's eyes.

Energetically, at your foundation, you and your partner are combining energies in your Root Chakras. The Root Chakra is dedicated to feeling safe and connected to the planet, giving you a sense of stability and home. This is why you feel a sense of home and calm when you are with your partner no matter where you are, or if you are having a fight with your partner, you may feel a sense of fear, distress, or being ungrounded.

When you are going through a breakup, and you have not released the energy cords from your Root Chakra to your partner's, you may get a sense of not having a home and not feeling stable because you have not re-established your Root as your own again. When you don't have a clear solid Root Chakra connection, you could feel lost or suicidal, as if you don't have a place or a home in the world. You might mistakenly think that the only way to feel peace again is to be with your former partner, but the truth is you just need to re-establish your own connection. Once you do this, you will have a more permanent experience of serenity.

The Root Chakra is located at your perineum, between your sexual organs and your anus. It appears as the color red and gives a sensation of being grounded, safe, and at home. This is the most physical of the chakras, and can help you have a feeling of being present and grounded in your body. If you are not fully activated in your Root Chakra, you may feel afraid, unsafe, weak, have trouble feeling present and grounded, and you might feel like you are floating from place to place, never feeling at home, even if you have a home.

When you are going through a breakup, oftentimes it may feel like you have been uprooted. During a relationship, you merge your energy with your partner. This helps you in many ways to accelerate your spiritual growth. You have more energy and more insight because you now have access to another person's life lessons and abilities. Just by being around that person you will start to accumulate information and assimilate their energetic frequency. When you are around another person long enough, you begin to act, see, and feel like them. You take on their patterns, insights, and ways of being because you are sharing the same life together. (This happens in all your interactions with others, but because you spend so much time and space with your romantic partner they imprint on you most strongly.)

When That Person Is No Longer in Your Life

When you separate from your partner, it's important to establish a new way of being in the world. Your brain has been trained to make plans and decisions with them in mind, and your body still has patterns of how to relate in the world as part of a couple. It takes a retraining of the mind, body, and energy field to feel a sense of balance. It is a re-membering of your energy, mind, and body. It's similar to sorting out house items when you are separating from a partner: "This toaster belongs to you, this book is mine," and so forth. The processes I am about to share with you will help you sort out your own energy from that of your former partner so you can feel complete and whole again.

When A Partner's Energy Is Still in Your Root Chakra

When you are with a partner, you merge your energies together. You feel stronger together because each person's energy amplifies, and you bond to one another. This is why couples that have been together for a long time can sometimes be telepathic or empathic with one another. They start to resonate with one another and amplify each other's thoughts, feelings, and emotions. It feels wonderful to be deeply connected to another person in this way. You can have a sense that someone knows you fully and completely. There may be a feeling that it doesn't matter where you are because if you are with this person, you are at home and as one. You can feel open, expansive, and free. It feels as though you are no longer alone on your journey.

During a breakup this feeling of a safe, grounded connection can become compromised. You may feel lost, abandoned, scattered, and like you are going to die.

Why do you feel abandoned?

When you merge energies with another person, your connection to your own grounding can sometimes get tied up with the other person via energetic cords. If you were seeking to feel safe and connected before the relationship, and through this relationship you found that sense of safety and home, the chances are good that you have been intertwined in their grounding cord. When the relationship ended, so did the specific way you had been connecting to the planet during that relationship. Now you are back to where you started, only it feels worse because you know what it's like to feel safe and grounded. Now that feeling is gone, and you feel like the only way to experience that feeling again is to be with that person. This is why some people are so desperate to get back together with a partner, but merging again with this person may not be possible. This may not make you whole again.

However, if we take the time to truly clear and untangle this person's energy from our Root Chakra, we will be able to establish our own connection to the Earth. In doing so we will feel a profound sense of grounded safety, even more so than when we were tied into the other person.

These are some of the warning signs that you are tied up in someone else's Root Chakra:

- **You feel as though you can't live without them.**
- **You get anxious when you are not with them or can't speak to them.**
- **You feel depressed when they are not around.**

During this time it might seem like this other person is the only way to feel safe again, but the truth is that you can establish your own connection. It is already there, you just need to clearly align and balance it. If you are ready to feel safe, grounded, and balanced again, take some time to do the following exercise.

Root Chakra

Find a comfortable place to rest. You want to be fully and completely relaxed to allow these suggestions flow through you and create the changes you wish to receive.

Now, take a deep breath, and let's begin.

Focusing on the top of your head and all the muscles in and around the top of your head. As you breathe into these muscles, allow them to release, relax, and let go.

Focusing on your face, breathe and relax into your face, allowing all the muscles in and around your face to deeply relax with each and every breath.

Moving to the back of your head now, breathe and relax all of the muscles in and around the back of your head. Allowing each and every breath to bring you deeper into relaxation.

Allowing this relaxation to move down into your neck and shoulders. Breathing into your neck and shoulders, feeling so good so relaxed as you take another deep breath, allowing these muscles to release, relax and let go.

Feeling this relaxation move down into your arms and hands as you continue to relax and breathe. Letting go of all stress and tension as you take another deep breath.

As you breathe even more deeply, notice the rise and fall of your chest with each and every inhale and exhale. Notice how much more relaxed you are becoming. Each and every breath bringing you deeper into relaxation.

Feel this relaxation moving into your back now as you breathe even more deeply, even more slowly. You are safe and you are loved. You are deeply supported in this and all moments. Continuing to relax and breathe.

Breathing down into your belly, relaxing into your belly. Allow it to open and soften with each and every breath.

Breathe down into your hips and all the muscles in and around your hips. Feeling so good, so relaxed.

Moving down into your bottom, allowing all these muscles to release, relax, and let go.

Moving your awareness down into your thighs, and all the muscles in and around your thighs, releasing, relaxing, and letting go.

Feel the relaxation moving down into your knees, and all the muscles in and around your knees, as you continue down into your shins and calves. Allow your shins, and calves to release, relax, and let go.

Moving down into your ankles, breathing into your ankles, allow them to release, relax, and let go.

Take another deep breath and moving down into your feet and toes. Allow the relaxation to flow into all the muscles in your feet and toes, and let your toes know that it's okay to relax.

Focus now on your perineum, the space in-between your genitals and your anus. This is the energetic space where you are connected to the Earth. It is called your Root Chakra because this is where you are rooted to the Earth, like the roots of a tree. When this energy center is functioning correctly you feel safe, whole, complete, trusting, grounded, and at home.

Take some time right now to breathe into this energy center. As you focus and breathe into this space, imagine a red flower opening down into the Earth. As this red flower opens, see rays coming out from it like a cone of light. Focus and breathe into this place until you can feel or see the light becoming steadier. Relaxing and breathing . . . opening. The more relaxed you are the easier it is . . . just remember to relax.

Settle down into this Root Chakra like a bird settling into a nest, allowing it to open, smoothly and effortlessly.

As you focus on your Root Chakra, I want you to notice if there are any energies that don't belong to you.

Do you see or feel any energies or cords that belong to anyone else?

Call upon your angels and guides to help assist you to release any energy or cords that are not yours.

Relax and open into this place, allowing all energies and cords to be released.

You may imagine these cords as long arms with hands at the end, where you are both holding on to each other. Breathe and relax into this connection and allow the hands to soften and open. Then give the hand

of the other person's cord to an angel or guide to bring it back to the person to whom it belongs. This angel will assist your former partner in integrating this energy back into his or her body. Your former partner will be okay; your job of needing to be a caregiver is over now. You can let this person go, knowing that a safe and whole future awaits them.

Take a deep breath. Know that you will be okay. You are fully and completely safe and supported in this and all moments, and it's okay to let your former partner go. You are doing an amazing service for both of you; both of you are returning to a state of wholeness and completion. As his or her energy is released from your body there will be more space for you in your body. You will feel a more pronounced state of peace and calm. The feeling of anxiousness or distress is only experienced when another person's energy cord is attached to you. Once this energy cord is gone completely, you will feel relief.

Scan your body and breathe out any energy you have taken on from this person. Anywhere you have been holding on to their energy in your body, breathe it back now. You don't need this energy anymore. It no longer serves you. As you release this energy back to them you will come to understand that your own energy and your connection to the Earth will give you so much more love, peace, and joy than the energy of this other person. If you find yourself not wanting to give up their energy, ask yourself why.

Are these energies and feelings really giving you peace?

Or by holding on to this energy, are you actually causing yourself and the other person needless suffering?

Continue to relax and breathe until you have released all the energy back to where it came from. You will know you are done when you feel calm, thoughts of them are gone, and you no longer see pictures of them in your head.

Now take some time to breath yourself back from wherever you have given your energy away. Just breathe in through your nose and imagine that all your energy is coming back from the other person's body, situations you have been in, places you have been, everywhere you have left energy. Breathe it back now into your body, cleansed and purified as it comes back to you. Breathe it all back inside you. Feel yourself settling fully and completely back into your body.

Take some time once again to really move into your root area. Feel yourself settle in fully and completely. Own this space. This is your connection to your body and the planet. Allow yourself to open up fully and completely, easily and effortlessly, opening, opening, opening. Feel yourself moving further and deeper into this place, feeling a sense of warmth, opening, safety, and of being at home. If there is any tension or resistance, continue to relax and open into it. Nothing can harm you here. You are safe and you are loved. Continue to relax and breathe.

Focusing on the base of your spine, send out two lines of energy or roots down the sides of your legs and into the earth. These lines of energy will help to stabilize you even further. Notice what it feels like to have this extra stabilizing force. Take another deep breath and go deeper into relaxation.

Imagine now a white-golden light filling up the space around you. This light clears away all that is not you and attracts only the highest vibrations of love and light.

As you breathe, this light penetrates every cell of your body. Light surrounds you, penetrates you, and fills you with a peaceful, loving feeling. You are light; you are love; you are infinite; you are so much more than enough.

Take a deep breath and take in this feeling, the feeling of your true self. You are a beautiful physical being of pure light.

Allow this light to expand around you and within you. You are safe and you are loved. You are complete and you are free.

Bring this light fully and completely into your body and allow it to flow into your feet. Feel the energy flowing from the top of your head down your body and into your feet. Feel yourself filling back into your body and occupying every cell.

Really own this physical body. Make it yours. Come back in until you feel completely full and completely at home.

CHAPTER 13

Remembering Your Passion And Creativity

Sacral Chakra

The Sacral Chakra is located about two inches below your belly button. It is the center for creativity, sensuality, and connection with others. This is the joy and pleasure center. The front aspect of the Sacral Chakra is for giving, creating, and doing. The rear aspect connects to the front aspect in the center of the body and shows how we receive from others.

When someone is a chronic giver, the front aspect of his or her chakra tends to be very open while the rear tends to be barely open or closed altogether. This represents someone who is able to give energy and love, but unable to receive it properly. That can be very frustrating for someone who gives all the time. They often end up getting burned out because their energy is not being replenished. Sometimes they blame the people around them for never giving to them, when in reality they are actually not able to receive the energy even if it is offered. They end up pushing away the energy if it does present itself because it feels too uncomfortable to receive with a closed chakra.

The function of a chakra depends not only on the chakra being open or closed, but also with how clear it is. When we are in a romantic relationship with another person, we share energy with them through our chakras. If we are sexually attracted to them, we are sending energy back and forth through our sacral chakra. If there are core beliefs regarding this chakra with either partner, you both will help each other work out these issues through acting out certain scenarios that will bring up issues to clear them. If you are both awake and aware this is happening, you can transmute the energy and issues. If neither of you is aware of the reasons behind what is happening, it will often be perceived as distracting drama, leaving you both wondering why this specific issue keeps coming up again and again in your relationships.

When we are going through a breakup, we may feel a strong sense of abandonment and vulnerability, sometimes even more than we would have expected. That is because much of the time these emotions are not all stemming from this particular partner, but are interlaced with painful memories and lessons from our past, perhaps from when we were very young.

We tend to go off the deep end when a part of us who is very young is triggered. At a young age, we were not able to handle feeling abandoned or abused. However, we don't always know that we are being triggered. We don't always understand that a younger aspect of ourselves is experiencing a reaction. Once we can identify that part of us, we can re-parent it. We can let that young child know that everything is okay, that we are not alone, and that the feelings we are having right now will ease in time. We can let our younger self know that we are here for her and we will take care of her, that she is safe and loved. Taking the time to comfort this part of ourselves can make all the difference in how quickly we can release and let go of a relationship, and perhaps we can even take this opportunity to heal deep, long-forgotten childhood wounds for good.

Our sacral chakra helps us to feel closer to others. When we have an open and free-flowing sacral chakra, we feel confident and happy. Our interactions with others feel friendly and relaxed. We tend to be more creative and to have a feeling of calmness, confidence, and sensuality. This makes us very attractive. When people are around someone with a strong sacral chakra, they tend to feel safe and secure.

When the sacral chakra is blocked, or is not working properly, there is a tendency towards clinging, grasping, and jealousy. You could be over- or under-sexualized. You might have difficulty connecting with others because of trust issues. You may have difficulty being creative, experiencing artist's or writer's block.

Sacral Chakra

Find a comfortable place to rest. You want to be fully and completely relaxed to allow these suggestions flow through you and create the changes you wish to receive.

Now, take a deep breath, and let's begin.

Focusing on the top of your head and all the muscles in and around the top of your head. As you breathe into these muscles, allow them to release, relax, and let go.

Focusing on your face, breathe and relax into your face, allowing all the muscles in and around your face to deeply relax with each and every breath.

Moving to the back of your head now, breathe and relax all of the muscles in and around the back of your head. Allowing each and every breath to bring you deeper into relaxation.

Allowing this relaxation to move down into your neck and shoulders. Breathing into your neck and shoulders, feeling so good so relaxed as you take another deep breath, allowing these muscles to release, relax and let go.

Feeling this relaxation move down into your arms and hands as you continue to relax and breathe. Letting go of all stress and tension as you take another deep breath.

As you breathe even more deeply, notice the rise and fall of your chest with each and every inhale and exhale. Notice how much more relaxed you are becoming. Each and every breath bringing you deeper into relaxation.

Feel this relaxation moving into your back now as you breathe even more deeply, even more slowly. You are safe and you are loved. You are deeply supported in this and all moments. Continuing to relax and breathe.

Breathing down into your belly, relaxing into your belly. Allow it to open and soften with each and every breath.

Breathe down into your hips and all the muscles in and around your hips. Feeling so good, so relaxed.

Moving down into your bottom, allowing all these muscles to release, relax, and let go.

Moving your awareness down into your thighs, and all the muscles in and around your thighs, releasing, relaxing, and letting go.

Feel the relaxation moving down into your knees, and all the muscles in and around your knees, as you continue down into your shins and calves. Allow your shins, and calves to release, relax, and let go.

Moving down into your ankles, breathing into your ankles, allow them to release, relax, and let go.

Take another deep breath and moving down into your feet and toes. Allow the relaxation to flow into all the muscles in your feet and toes, and let your toes know that it's okay to relax.

Focusing on your sacral chakra, located about two fingers down from your belly button, breathe in. Allow yourself to relax and open.

What are you feeling here?

Do you feel energy that doesn't belong to you?

Gently breathe into this area and allow it to loosen and release.

Now, as you breathe out, imagine this energy going back to whomever it belongs to. It could be many people. Keep breathing and relaxing into this place until it feels clear of all energy that is not yours.

Imagine all the energy that you have given away to others coming back to you with your in breath. Continue breathing out other people's energy and breathing in all the energy you have given away to others.

Notice if there are energy cords here. If you feel an energy cord, find its root inside of you. Sometimes it looks like a hand holding another hand. Sometimes it looks like tree roots. You will see or sense the cord in your own way, but when you locate it, unravel the roots or the fingers that are holding on to each other. Gently and easily give away the other person's cord to an angel or guide to bring back to where it belongs.

The more you relax during this process, the easier it will be. After the cord has been released, put your hand on the area it was released from and, using your intention, fill it with your own energy and light. Imagine all the empty dark places being filled with your own love, energy, and light interweaving together to make this place strong, whole, and complete.

When the front aspect of the Sacral Chakra is complete, then move into the rear aspect. Allow yourself to relax and open as you focus in this place. Ask for the rear Sacral Chakra to be cleared, aligned, balanced, and strengthened. This is where you are open to receive sexual and sensual feelings, creative ideas, and money, so if this chakra is closed or clogged, you will

want to clear it to let in all the good stuff! If you notice any places that feel stuck, tight, or struggling, breathe into them and allow them to open, relax, and clear.

Follow the same steps of loosening energy cords and returning energy to where it belongs as with the frontal Sacral Chakra.

Put your hand on the chakra and use your intention to fill it with your own energy and light. Imagine all the empty dark places being filled with your own love, energy, and light, interweaving together to make this place strong, whole, and complete.

Imagine now a white-golden light filling up the space around you. This light clears away all that is not you and attracts only the highest vibrations of love and light.

As you breathe, this light penetrates every cell of your body. Light surrounds you, penetrates you, and fills you with a peaceful, loving feeling. You are light; you are love; you are infinite; you are so much more than enough.

Take a deep breath and take in this feeling, the feeling of your true self. You are a beautiful physical being of pure light. Allow this light to expand around you and within you. You are safe and you are loved. You are complete and you are free.

Bring this light fully and completely into your body and allow it to flow into your feet. Feel the energy flowing from the top of your head down your body and into your feet. Feel yourself filling back into your body and occupying every cell.

Really own this physical body. Make it yours. Come back in until you feel completely full and completely at home.

CHAPTER 14

Reclaiming Your Power

Solar Plexus Chakra

Have you ever felt like you are in a power struggle with a partner? Maybe you have given away all your power to them, or they have given it away to you or you are both fighting for dominance. Perhaps you are both fighting to be taken care of and/or dominated.

The solar plexus is the center of our power. It is where we show up in the world with all we have. When we give our energy away to another person it feels like all our energy goes toward making that person happy, toward figuring out how to be a better partner for them. It is wonderful to care about your partner, but when all your time and energy is focused on them, it becomes smothering and stifling for them. This person fell in love with you because of who you truly are, what you enjoy, and the way you express yourself in the world. When you leave *your true self* behind to become a people-pleaser, you stop being the person you are and your partner may become bored with the person you have become, mostly because you are not your unique self anymore. Instead, you are someone who is wishy-washy, second-guessing your actions and thoughts to please your partner. We are never able to please another person fully and completely. We can never know exactly what they want because it can change from moment to moment.

What if being in a relationship is about learning about the other person's uniqueness and finding interesting things about them?

What if they want to please you as much as you want to please them?

If you are constantly giving, there is no room for your partner to give to you. And vice versa: If you keep taking all the time and never giving back, your partner will eventually get tired, feel the imbalance, and wish for a partnership with more of an exchange of energy.

Balancing this chakra will help you to feel more fully in your power, where the give and take of energy is in balance. You can be in charge, and you can give up control easily and effortlessly without struggle because you know where your power lies. You don't need to get approval from another person and you don't need to dominate them. You simply know who you are and feel confident in being you.

Solar Plexus Chakra

Find a comfortable place to rest. You want to be fully and completely relaxed to allow these suggestions flow through you and create the changes you wish to receive.

Now, take a deep breath, and let's begin.

Focusing on the top of your head and all the muscles in and around the top of your head. As you breathe into these muscles, allow them to release, relax, and let go.

Focusing on your face, breathe and relax into your face, allowing all the muscles in and around your face to deeply relax with each and every breath.

Moving to the back of your head now, breathe and relax all of the muscles in and around the back of your head. Allowing each and every breath to bring you deeper into relaxation.

Allowing this relaxation to move down into your neck and shoulders. Breathing into your neck and shoulders, feeling so good so relaxed as you take another deep breath, allowing these muscles to release, relax and let go.

Feeling this relaxation move down into your arms and hands as you continue to relax and breathe. Letting go of all stress and tension as you take another deep breath.

As you breathe even more deeply, notice the rise and fall of your chest with each and every inhale and exhale. Notice how much more relaxed you are becoming. Each and every breath bringing you deeper into relaxation.

Feel this relaxation moving into your back now as you breathe even more deeply, even more slowly. You are safe and you are loved. You are deeply supported in this and all moments. Continuing to relax and breathe.

Breathing down into your belly, relaxing into your belly. Allow it to open and soften with each and every breath.

Breathe down into your hips and all the muscles in and around your hips. Feeling so good, so relaxed.

Moving down into your bottom, allowing all these muscles to release, relax, and let go.

Moving your awareness down into your thighs, and all the muscles in and around your thighs, releasing, relaxing, and letting go.

Feel the relaxation moving down into your knees, and all the muscles in and around your knees, as you continue down into your shins and calves. Allow your shins, and calves to release, relax, and let go.

Moving down into your ankles, breathing into your ankles, allow them to release, relax, and let go.

Take another deep breath and moving down into your feet and toes. Allow the relaxation to flow into all the muscles in your feet and toes, and let your toes know that it's okay to relax.

Breathe now into the front aspect of your Solar Plexus Chakra, located right at your diaphragm. It may feel anxious or tight. Whatever feelings you discover are okay. Just breathe into them and acknowledge what you are feeling. Remember now that you are an eternal being and your natural state of being is calm, peaceful, and loving. If you are feeling anything other than these emotions, they do not belong to you. This is why they feel so uncomfortable.

Sometimes these feelings are part of a painful story we have been telling ourselves, sometimes it's someone else's story. These feelings are trying to show you where you are not clear, and as you tune into them, you can thank them for their lesson and release them from your body.

Tune in again to the feelings in your diaphragm.

As you identify these feelings, ask, "Who does this belong to?"

"Does this belong to me?"

If it feels heavy when you ask that question, then it's time to release this energy back to wherever or whomever you took it from.

As you tune in deeper, ask yourself who or what you are trying to control. If you are trying to control situations or the way other people act or react, it results in pain, because there is nothing you can truly do about the actions of others. At times, you may get a feeling as if you need to control everything in your world in order for you to feel safe. But in actuality, you may come to realize that you never feel quite safe, because there is always one more thing you have to control.

The way to truly feel safe and at ease is to give up the need to control. It might seem counterintuitive, but as you let go, it gives the universe a chance to fill in the gaps of what you are looking for. You are only able to receive your dream life and partner when you open your hands and your heart. When you are trying to control, you are grasping, holding tightly, and you can't receive anything new because your hands are clenched onto the past. The only way you can embrace the now and welcome the future good that wants to come to you is to relax into the pain and open to receive the good that is coming.

Tune into all those places that are tight and struggling and relax into them. Slow down your breath and relax even further. As you relax into these places, what do you notice? Keep breathing and relaxing until you feel clear and complete.

After you are done clearing the front aspect of the Solar Plexus Chakra, move to the rear aspect. As you tune into it notice any tightness or places that are struggling, and breathe into them. As you open this rear aspect of the solar plexus, you are opening yourself up to receive your power and will from Source energy.

Allow yourself to completely open this chakra and clear all energies that don't belong to you. Feel into them and breathe out the energy that does not belong to you, sending it back to whomever you took it on from. Relax into this place more deeply. Filling in the places that were occupied with other people's energy with your own.

Is there a core belief that you need to get your power from another person?

We call up that core belief to be cleared and released. We dissolve this core belief and any contracts or agreements associated with it. We are shifting into a new vibrational frequency, restructuring, and recalibrating to a higher frequency. Continue opening, relaxing, breathing, and opening more, clearing into a higher frequency, harmonizing and stabilizing.

Imagine now a white-golden light filling up the space around you. This light clears away all that is not you and attracts only the highest vibrations of love and light.

As you breathe, this light penetrates every cell of your body. Light surrounds you, penetrates you, and fills you with a peaceful, loving feeling. You are light; you are love; you are infinite; you are so much more than enough.

Take a deep breath and take in this feeling, the feeling of your true self. You are a beautiful physical being of pure light. Allow this light to expand around you and within you. You are safe and you are loved. You are complete and you are free.

Bring this light fully and completely into your body and allow it to flow into your feet. Feel the energy flowing from the top of your head down your body and into your feet. Feel yourself filling back into your body and occupying every cell.

Really own this physical body. Make it yours. Come back in until you feel completely full and completely at home.

This session is now complete and your Sacral Chakra will continue to integrate this energy for the next three days. Be gentle with yourself during this process of unfolding.

CHAPTER 15

Opening Your Heart and Trusting Love Again

The Heart Chakra

When we are born, we are in a state of love and connection. We are trusting of people and the world around us. But the adults who take care of us have been through trials and tribulations. They were not always in a state of love and understanding, and frequently are in a state of being tired or forgetful. Our parents probably have said or done something that caused us pain when we were young.

When someone we love causes us pain, our heart tries to protect itself by creating an energetic heart wall. Heart walls are created with layers of painful emotions that have had an impact on us and have stuck to us. Sometimes we can have years' worth of layers surrounding our hearts, accumulated from different experiences. This makes it difficult to love others and to feel love, because the love that is being received and given goes through this filter of stuck emotions. That can cause us a lot of pain, which can cause our hearts to restrict the flow of energy through the Heart Chakra, the place where we give and receive love.

When we are in a state of pain, we have forgotten that we are love and everyone else around us is love, too. We have forgotten that every situation is an opportunity to lead us back to love. When we choose to believe something other than love is at play in any situation, we usually experience pain.

The pain we feel is occurring because our heart naturally wants to be open and trusting. Our heart always wants to be in a state of allowing the flow of love, and wants to include everyone in that loving. So, the act of trying to close it, to exclude people from our lives and not experience love, is painful, both emotionally and sometimes even physically. It's like trying to hold back a river; it takes a lot of energy not to be in a state of love.

Love is our natural state of being. Love is essentially who we are. When we are feeling love, it opens us up to the flow of the joy and energy that is always around us. Love attracts more love. When we are loving, we attract more loving situations because we are vibrationally and energetically a match.

It is a challenge to question our feelings when we are hurting. We think we are justified. We think that "they" deserve to pay, and by having these hurtful feelings that somehow we will be vindicated. But this is just our ego, or pain body, trying to make sense of what is going on. It is trying to keep us "safe," but following the direction of our pain body or ego will only bring more pain. Even though it may feel like a contradiction of what is true, you need to release the need to be right and to protect yourself if you want to feel love and be free again.

The safest thing you can do is open your heart again and to remember that you are love, and that there is *only* love in this situation. The person who seems to be hurting you is also love, even if they might be in a state of forgetting, too. Opening to love doesn't mean that you open yourself up to the person who has been hurting you, in fact sometimes the most loving thing you can do for yourself and that other person is to walk away so neither of you has to experience the cycle of disharmony you are creating and recreating.

Once you are free of the other person you can choose to forgive yourself for what has happened and eventually forgive the other person for the role they had in causing pain. But how do you forgive someone when you are holding onto resentment, anger, shame or guilt?

Ho'oponopono

I'm sorry

Please forgive me

I love you

Thank you

This is the beautiful ancient Hawaiian forgiveness practice called Ho'ponopono. Ho'o(Make)Pono(Right)Pono(Right) Roughly translated as making things right for them and you…creating a win win situation out of something that might seem hopeless.

When you say the words of the Ho'oponopono with as much feeling as you can, the words go in and heal the situation. How is that possible? There are a few reasons why.

Have you ever been in an argument and wished the other person would just say they were sorry? If they would just say they were sorry then you could just both go on and live your lives again. But you aren't going to forgive them unless they say it, because you really need to hear those words before forgiveness can happen and you can move on. Maybe what you really want is to feel loved. You are so sad that person is mad at you or you had the fight and you really just want them to love you again and you have no idea how that is going to happen.

Maybe you feel sorry and you wish you could make things better, but the more you try to speak to them and fix things, the worse things seem to get and the more upset they get with you.

As you say the words of the Ho'oponopono you put the words in between you and the other person and the words that were unsaid begin to infuse and diffuse the tension of the relationship. The vibration of the spoken words and even the thought of them will begin to shift the frequency and vibration of the situation. Remember, you words and your intention are extremely powerful. They can harm or heal a situation. There have been different experiments done on this to show the power of words and intention.

Dr. Masaru Emoto of Japan did experiments where he put regular tap water into jars. For some of the jars he focused loving thoughts or said loving words. For other jars he thought or spoke hateful and angry words. Then he would freeze the sample waters. What he found was that the loving happy thoughts produced beautiful water crystals, while the hateful thoughts produced ugly malformed water crystals. The water "remembered" the words and vibrations in the water crystals. Why is this important? Our body is made up of 60% water. So if thoughts and intentions can shift water molecules, imagine what they are doing to our body.

http://www.masaru-emoto.net/english/water-crystal.html

Also, as you are saying the words I'm sorry, please forgive me, I love you, thank you, there is a relaxing that begins to happen in your being. Instead of holding on tight to being right, trying to fix things, wanting them to see your point of view or see you in a different light, you begin to loosen your grip on the situation. The importance and focus shift to forgiveness and peace instead of the pain of trying to change someone else's thoughts or feelings from a lower vibrational place.

Coming back to love when you are in pain might be the most challenging and courageous choice you can ever make. I believe that if we want to live in a loving world, it is something we all need to choose . . . for our own sake and for the sake of the world.

Heart Chakra

Find a comfortable place to rest. You want to be fully and completely relaxed to allow these suggestions flow through you and create the changes you wish to receive.

Now, take a deep breath, and let's begin.

Focusing on the top of your head and all the muscles in and around the top of your head. As you breathe into these muscles, allow them to release, relax, and let go.

Focusing on your face, breathe and relax into your face, allowing all the muscles in and around your face to deeply relax with each and every breath.

Moving to the back of your head now, breathe and relax all of the muscles in and around the back of your head. Allowing each and every breath to bring you deeper into relaxation.

Allowing this relaxation to move down into your neck and shoulders. Breathing into your neck and shoulders, feeling so good so relaxed as you take another deep breath, allowing these muscles to release, relax and let go.

Feeling this relaxation move down into your arms and hands as you continue to relax and breathe. Letting go of all stress and tension as you take another deep breath.

As you breathe even more deeply, notice the rise and fall of your chest with each and every inhale and exhale. Notice how much more relaxed you are becoming. Each and every breath bringing you deeper into relaxation.

Feel this relaxation moving into your back now as you breathe even more deeply, even more slowly. You are safe and you are loved. You are deeply supported in this and all moments. Continuing to relax and breathe.

Breathing down into your belly, relaxing into your belly. Allow it to open and soften with each and every breath.

Breathe down into your hips and all the muscles in and around your hips. Feeling so good, so relaxed.

Moving down into your bottom, allowing all these muscles to release, relax, and let go.

Moving your awareness down into your thighs, and all the muscles in and around your thighs, releasing, relaxing, and letting go.

Feel the relaxation moving down into your knees, and all the muscles in and around your knees, as you continue down into your shins and calves. Allow your shins, and calves to release, relax, and let go.

Moving down into your ankles, breathing into your ankles, allow them to release, relax, and let go.

Take another deep breath and moving down into your feet and toes. Allow the relaxation to flow into all the muscles in your feet and toes, and let your toes know that it's okay to relax.

Focus now on your Heart Chakra . . . feel into it and breathe into it.

As you focus and relax into your Heart Chakra, does it feel uncomfortable?

Notice if there is any energy here that does not belong to you. If your answer is yes, feel deeply into the sensations, and breathe the energy back to the person it belongs to. Keep feeling deeper into the uncomfortable feelings, remembering that there is only discomfort because this energy is not yours or it is a thought that is not truthful or loving. Once you clear it out, you will begin to feel much more relaxed. Keep breathing the energy out and moving deeper into yourself. Settle into the places that have been occupied by this outside energy. Keep breathing and releasing.

Is there fear?

Do you feel sadness or grief?

Does it belong to you or someone else?

Using your intention, release the energy of these uncomfortable feelings back to where they came from.

Move into these places gently and nurture them, letting them know that you are safe and you are loved.

Do you notice any energy cords in the area of your Heart Chakra?

Call in an angel or guide to take each energy cord back to whomever it belongs. Breathe and relax into the root of the cord. Allow it to loosen up and release and give the end to an angel or guide. As you relax and exhale through your mouth, release any energy residue left in your Heart Chakra back to who ever you took it on from. Now relax and inhale all energy that belongs to you from the other person in through your nose.

Now breathe into the Heart Chakra and fill it up with your own energy and love. Filling every space with your own loving energy.

Now focus on the space around the Heart Chakra.

Is there a Heart Wall?

If so, direct your attention here, and relax. Call in your angels and guides to assist in releasing the emotions that are creating this wall.

I am going to give you a list of emotions. Allow each of these to be dissolved on a quantum level. No matter how many times they are repeated or have shown up and have been layered in, allow them to be dissolved and released. May your heart shift in frequency as this happens, allowing for the new vibration of love to enter. Ask for this to happen quickly, safely, and easily.

Again, all emotions are cleared an infinite number of times until gone. Let's begin with what you are feeling:

Clearing all feelings of:

Abandonment
Alienation
Anger
Anxiety
Betrayal
Bitterness
Blamed and blaming
Conflict
Confusion
Defensive
Despair
Discouragement
Disgust
Dread
Failure
Lack of self-esteem
Longing
Lost
Lust
Manic
Nervousness
Overwhelmed
Peeved
Pride
Rejection
Resentment
Sadness
Self-abuse
Shame
Shock

Fear
Forlorn
Grief
Guilt
Hatred
Heartache
Helplessness
Hopelessness
Horror
Humiliation
Insecurity
Jealousness
Sorrow
Stubbornness
Terror
Unappreciated
Unloved
Unworthy
Vulnerability
Weepy
Wishy-washy
Worried
Worthless

Imagine a river of crystalline light flowing through your Heart Chakra...the healing waters are clearing any leftover residue in, through, and around the heart. This beautiful healing water not only cleanses the heart but it is raising the frequency and making the heart feel much lighter and full of joy.

Continue by grounding and integrating new energetic frequencies, and harmonizing the Heart Chakra with higher frequencies.

Feel deeper into your Heart Chakra.

Are there any places that are still holding on, still stuck?

Allow yourself to sink into them with love. Let them know you are safe and you are loved, and it's okay. Just breathe and relax, and know that everything is unfolding in Divine timing.

Move now into the rear aspect of the Heart Chakra. This is where you open to receive love.

As you breathe into this place, does it feel tight or restricted?

Relax and breathe into this energy.

Are there any energy cords here?

Take the time now to breathe into this energy and release all the energy that is not yours back to the person it belongs to, in the same way that you cleared the front aspect of the Heart Chakra, exhaling the energy cords that belong to others, and inhaling your own energy from wherever it may be.

Call in crystal healing waters to wash away any leftover energy that might need clearing, this will clear and raise the frequency of the Heart Chakra.

Imagine now a white-golden light filling up the space around you. This light clears away all that is not you and attracts only the highest vibrations of love and light.

As you breathe, this light penetrates every cell of your body. Light surrounds you, penetrates you, and fills you with a peaceful, loving feeling. You are light; you are love; you are infinite; you are so much more than enough.

Take a deep breath and take in this feeling, the feeling of your true self. You are a beautiful physical being of pure light. Allow this light to expand around you and within you. You are safe and you are loved. You are complete and you are free.

Bring this light fully and completely into your body and allow it to flow into your feet. Feel the energy flowing from the top of your head down your body and into your feet.

Feel yourself filling back into your body and occupying every cell.

Really own this physical body. Make it yours. Come back in until you feel completely full and completely at home.

This session is now over, but your heart will keep integrating, clearing, and opening over the next three days as you get used to the new frequencies. Be gentle with yourself while the healing unfolds, and give yourself as much time as you need to adjust to this new feeling of love.

Chapter 16

Speaking Your Truth

Throat Chakra

Do you find yourself wondering what you believe now that you are no longer part of a couple?

Are you still saying things you and your partner used to say?

Do you find yourself wanting to say "we" instead of "I"?

In relationship, these pronouns sometimes become entangled in the things that we do and think and say. We merge our truths together. Then, they become a combination of what we believe and what our partner believes until we sometimes forget our own outlook on the world. It's not always a bad thing: we can learn from other people's points of view and ways of being.

But sometimes when we are releasing a partner we forget what our point of view is without the other person and we feel despair, thinking: "Who am I if I am not with them?"

It is important to recognize the contributions that this person has made to our lives, how they have shaped the way we think and communicate in the world, and how we have shaped the way they see the world, as well. We can be thankful for the ways they helped us to grow and experience life in different ways. We can take the parts we love and incorporate them into our being as our own, and we can let go of the things that are not serving us anymore.

We are receiving lessons from every person we meet and incorporating what we learn into our being. This person just happened to be in our life in a more concentrated way, so it seems like a more intense task to sort out. You can do this. This part of the program is about remembering who you are.

Remember: you are constantly changing and growing. The person you were before this relationship is not who you are now. You will not be the same five years from now or ten years from now. The only thing you can really count on is that things are constantly changing. The fact that you might not think you know who you are right now is a good thing. It is time to get curious.

Get quiet and ask your body, "What do you like right now?"

"What kind of music do you like right now?"

"What kinds of movies do you want to see right now?"

"What kind of food do you like right now?"

When you are quiet and check in with yourself, you may find that the answers surprise you.

This is a wonderful time for you to get to know your body again. Your body is your soul mate. It is the perfect mate for your soul. It is the reason you get to be here this lifetime. The easiest way to get to know this is to start a new conversation with it. In the quiet times ask your body questions.

Ask your body what it likes, how you can be a better friend to it.

What does your body want you to know?

Use your hands and touch your naked body all over.

What does it feel like?

What doesn't it feel like?

Where is your body numb?

Take some time to awaken those places by gently putting your presence there. Give each part of your body love. And if touching your body is uncomfortable for you, ask yourself why.

Why is it wrong for you to touch your own body?

Do you have any thoughts or beliefs about it being okay for someone else to touch your body?

Question where your belief comes from and ask yourself if you would really like to hold on to that belief anymore.

I remember a time with my first boyfriend when we were lying in bed and the sun was going down. We watched the sunset and the stars come out. It felt like a magical time full of peace and happiness. I remember thinking years later that I wished I had a boyfriend so I could experience that feeling again. Then it dawned on me: I didn't need a partner to experience that. I did not need to wait for someone else to come into my life to lie in bed and watch the sunset! So that night I created a date night with myself. I took off all my clothes, got in bed early, put my favorite music on, and watched the sunset and stars come out.

I remember thinking, "Wow, why did I wait so long to do this?"

Our experiences, how we feel, our outlook on life—all these come from us. It might seem as if they are happening because of another person, but we are mostly using that person to give us permission to feel and do the things we want to do. The experiences and the feelings are purely our own. They come from within.

Throat Chakra

Find a comfortable place to rest. You want to be fully and completely relaxed to allow these suggestions flow through you and create the changes you wish to receive.

Now, take a deep breath, and let's begin.

Focusing on the top of your head and all the muscles in and around the top of your head. As you breathe into these muscles, allow them to release, relax, and let go.

Focusing on your face, breathe and relax into your face, allowing all the muscles in and around your face to deeply relax with each and every breath.

Moving to the back of your head now, breathe and relax all of the muscles in and around the back of your head. Allowing each and every breath to bring you deeper into relaxation.

Allowing this relaxation to move down into your neck and shoulders. Breathing into your neck and shoulders, feeling so good so relaxed as you take another deep breath, allowing these muscles to release, relax and let go.

Feeling this relaxation move down into your arms and hands as you continue to relax and breathe. Letting go of all stress and tension as you take another deep breath.

As you breathe even more deeply, notice the rise and fall of your chest with each and every inhale and exhale. Notice how much more relaxed you are becoming. Each and every breath bringing you deeper into relaxation.

Feel this relaxation moving into your back now as you breathe even more deeply, even more slowly. You are safe and you are loved. You are deeply supported in this and all moments. Continuing to relax and breathe.

Breathing down into your belly, relaxing into your belly. Allow it to open and soften with each and every breath.

Breathe down into your hips and all the muscles in and around your hips. Feeling so good, so relaxed.

Moving down into your bottom, allowing all these muscles to release, relax, and let go.

Moving your awareness down into your thighs, and all the muscles in and around your thighs, releasing, relaxing, and letting go.

Feel the relaxation moving down into your knees, and all the muscles in and around your knees, as you continue down into your shins and calves. Allow your shins, and calves to release, relax, and let go.

Moving down into your ankles, breathing into your ankles, allow them to release, relax, and let go.

Take another deep breath and moving down into your feet and toes. Allow the relaxation to flow into all the muscles in your feet and toes, and let your toes know that it's okay to relax.

Focus now into your Throat Chakra.

Does it feel tight or restricted?

Is there energy or beliefs you have taken on from others that are keeping you from being able to speak your truth?

Feel into this dissonant energy. Breathe into it. Allow yourself to relax into these places and begin to release the uncomfortable energy that feels out of place, exhaling it out through your mouth. As you breathe it out, you might also use a tone or a sound. Whatever comes out is okay, just keep breathing and releasing this energy. Your body knows exactly how and what you need to do to release it all, so just relax and trust and keep breathing.

Are there any beliefs from others located in your Throat Chakra?

The Throat Chakra is a place of truth, and sometimes we take on other people's truths.

Is there someone else's truth here that you need to give back to them?

Be honest: Is this truth still serving you?

If you get a no, then let's release it back to whomever you took it on from. Feel deeply into it . . . relax into it.

However, you might have bought into this belief as your own, we dissolve it down to the root now. Relax into it, bringing up any agreements and contracts holding it in place. Go back to the original soul agreement that is holding this truth in place, clearing and dissolving all remnants that are no longer needed.

In the place of these beliefs, you now integrate a new frequency and higher vibration. This applies to all foreign belief structures that are not serving you in this present time, and to past, present, and future incarnations.

Now bring the Throat Chakra to the present incarnation, and shift from child to adult energy frequency. Bring all energies up to the present moment.

Integrate all changes, harmonizing new frequencies and vibrations. Bring all aspects to present moment.

This session is now complete. Energies will continue to integrate, harmonize, and clear for the next three days, so be gentle with yourself.

CHAPTER 17

Trusting Your Insights

Third Eye Chakra

The Third Eye Chakra is the place where we receive insights, both into ourselves and into others. When it is clear and open we know who we are and what we want to do and be in the world. We can also read other people clearly and easily. We know not only where they are coming from energetically and emotionally, but we have an understanding about the true essence of their being.

Sometimes, however, our Third Eye Chakra is clouded with other people's thoughts, feelings, and points of view. It may be our parents, friends, family, or society in general. Throughout our lives, our filters become cloudy, and it's hard to differentiate between what we are feeling and what we are picking up from others.

When extreme emotions come up that you can't seem to shift, ask yourself, "Who does this belong to? Does this emotion belong to me or someone else?"

You might be surprised to learn that you were just being empathic to someone else's feelings, or that someone was thinking of you, had those feelings, and was projecting them onto you.

Our natural inclination is to run away energetically from painful feelings, but if we do, the energy will still be present once we get back into our body. It might seem counterintuitive, but in order to release the feelings for good, we must go into them—feel them completely—in order to be free of them.

Here is a more detailed example of how to clear yourself of other people's thoughts, feelings, and emotions.

Clearing Other People's Energy

Get quiet and centered. Focus into the feelings and then expand yourself gently into that space. Relax into them and expand, then, through the mouth, exhale the thoughts and feelings out of your body. Breathe yourself back in through your nostrils and breathe all other people's energies out through your mouth.

Keep moving inward, into the places that feel scared or sad or stuck, and simply relax into them. Embody the spaces that feel tight or stuck and breathe . . . expand . . . relax. Continue to do this until you feel at peace.

Third Eye Chakra

Find a comfortable place to rest. You want to be fully and completely relaxed to allow these suggestions flow through you and create the changes you wish to receive.

Now, take a deep breath, and let's begin.

Focusing on the top of your head and all the muscles in and around the top of your head. As you breathe into these muscles, allow them to release, relax, and let go.

Focusing on your face, breathe and relax into your face, allowing all the muscles in and around your face to deeply relax with each and every breath.

Moving to the back of your head now, breathe and relax all of the muscles in and around the back of your head. Allowing each and every breath to bring you deeper into relaxation.

Allowing this relaxation to move down into your neck and shoulders. Breathing into your neck and shoulders, feeling so good so relaxed as you take another deep breath, allowing these muscles to release, relax and let go.

Feeling this relaxation move down into your arms and hands as you continue to relax and breathe. Letting go of all stress and tension as you take another deep breath.

As you breathe even more deeply, notice the rise and fall of your chest with each and every inhale and exhale. Notice how much more relaxed you are becoming. Each and every breath bringing you deeper into relaxation.

Feel this relaxation moving into your back now as you breathe even more deeply, even more slowly. You are safe and you are loved. You are deeply supported in this and all moments. Continuing to relax and breathe.

Breathing down into your belly, relaxing into your belly. Allow it to open and soften with each and every breath.

Breathe down into your hips and all the muscles in and around your hips. Feeling so good, so relaxed.

Moving down into your bottom, allowing all these muscles to release, relax, and let go.

Moving your awareness down into your thighs, and all the muscles in and around your thighs, releasing, relaxing, and letting go.

Feel the relaxation moving down into your knees, and all the muscles in and around your knees, as you continue down into your shins and calves. Allow your shins, and calves to release, relax, and let go.

Moving down into your ankles, breathing into your ankles, allow them to release, relax, and let go.

Take another deep breath and moving down into your feet and toes. Allow the relaxation to flow into all the muscles in your feet and toes, and let your toes know that it's okay to relax.

Focus now on your Third Eye Chakra.

Does it feel tight or blocked in any way?

Do you feel any pressure?

Breathe and relax into it. Allow all the blocks to come to the surface and breathe into them. Now return any of the energy, thoughts, or feelings you have taken on from others back to them. Relax, feel into them, and breathe them out through your mouth. Your intention is that this energy is taken back to whomever you took it on from, with love and consciousness. Give thanks that this perspective helped you for as long as it did, but acknowledge that it's now time to see with your own Third Eye and with your own point of view. Notice if there are any cords to beliefs or people holding them in place. If so relax and release these cords back to the people they belong to or give them to Divine Source energy.

Keep breathing and relaxing, allowing all the energy and cords that are not yours to be released. Move deeper into your Third Eye Chakra and settle into this place fully and completely.

Moving into the rear aspect of the Third Eye, clearing all the past blocks so that you can see the past more clearly. Releasing and clearing any family or ancestral truths or beliefs that are uncomfortable or not resonating with you anymore.

Harmonizing a new frequency and a new vibration in your clear and light-filled Third Eye Chakra.

CHAPTER 18

Connecting to Your Source

Crown Chakra

Our Crown Chakra is where we connect into our Divine Source Energy. It is where we feel at one with God, the Universe, Divine Source and the Ultimate Loving Energy that creates everything.

Sometimes during a breakup we feel like we have lost our connection to Divinity. It feels as if we have lost our very connection to God, the Universe, or whatever you call communion with All that is. It can feel absolutely devastating to believe that being with that person is the only way we will ever feel whole and connected again, that it is the only time we will ever feel open and free to receive Ultimate Love.

When we are in our body, fully grounded, and have our own connection to Divinity, there is a cord of energy going straight up to connect with Source energy from the top of our head. This comes from our Crown Chakra. When this connection is strong and resonant, we feel at peace, expansive, and open.

When we meet another person that we are infatuated with and fall in love with them, this connection expands even more and opens us even more deeply to Divinity. The problem comes in when we misidentify and misapply this person's love for Divine Love. We begin to believe that this person is the reason for Divine connection, and our own Divine connection moves from direct to filtering through the other person. It can feel good for a while to share the same view of life with another, to be so in tune and connected with them that you feel as One. But eventually you become dependent on that connection and that person. You forget that you have your own personal connection to the Divine, and when you forget your connection, you can feel lost and alone.

When you feel like you have lost your faith or when you experience more doubts than before, it is important to reestablish your own connection to the Divine. Once you do this you will feel at peace again.

Crown Chakra

Find a comfortable place to rest. You want to be fully and completely relaxed to allow these suggestions flow through you and create the changes you wish to receive.

Now, take a deep breath, and let's begin.

Focusing on the top of your head and all the muscles in and around the top of your head. As you breathe into these muscles, allow them to release, relax, and let go.

Focusing on your face, breathe and relax into your face, allowing all the muscles in and around your face to deeply relax with each and every breath.

Moving to the back of your head now, breathe and relax all of the muscles in and around the back of your head. Allowing each and every breath to bring you deeper into relaxation.

Allowing this relaxation to move down into your neck and shoulders. Breathing into your neck and shoulders, feeling so good so relaxed as you take another deep breath, allowing these muscles to release, relax and let go.

Feeling this relaxation move down into your arms and hands as you continue to relax and breathe. Letting go of all stress and tension as you take another deep breath.

As you breathe even more deeply, notice the rise and fall of your chest with each and every inhale and exhale. Notice how much more relaxed you are becoming. Each and every breath bringing you deeper into relaxation.

Feel this relaxation moving into your back now as you breathe even more deeply, even more slowly. You are safe and you are loved. You are deeply supported in this and all moments. Continuing to relax and breathe.

Breathing down into your belly, relaxing into your belly. Allow it to open and soften with each and every breath.

Breathe down into your hips and all the muscles in and around your hips. Feeling so good, so relaxed.

Moving down into your bottom, allowing all these muscles to release, relax, and let go.

Moving your awareness down into your thighs, and all the muscles in and around your thighs, releasing, relaxing, and letting go.

Feel the relaxation moving down into your knees, and all the muscles in and around your knees, as you continue down into your shins and calves. Allow your shins, and calves to release, relax, and let go.

Moving down into your ankles, breathing into your ankles, allow them to release, relax, and let go.

Take another deep breath and moving down into your feet and toes. Allow the relaxation to flow into all the muscles in your feet and toes, and let your toes know that it's okay to relax.

Tune in to your Crown Chakra.

Does it feel open and free or is there some energy in there that is not yours?

Breathe into any energy that feels heavy or restricting. Allow that energy to go back to whomever it belongs to . . . breathe it out through your mouth. Keep breathing it out until it feels completely freed.

Do you notice any core beliefs here?

Sometimes beliefs get stuck here that cause us pain or fear. If you feel any pain or fear, release those beliefs back to where you first found them. Your true nature is love. If you are feeling anything other than love, that means that it's not yours or it's not truthful for you and it's not working for your highest good. Release this energy now. Give thanks that it has helped you for as long as it has, but it is no longer for your highest good, so you release it in love. Breathe into any core beliefs and energies that are not yours and release them all back to where they came from.

Are there any energy cords present?

Breathe into your Crown Chakra and release any energy cords present here. Breathe and relax into the connections. We call upon angels and guides to take these energy cords back to whomever they belong to. You might feel fear or sadness come up. This is okay; just know that the person whose energy cord you are releasing will find their own connection, one that is more sustainable, and so will you. Each one of us here on the planet has a unique connection that gives us all the energy, information, and love that we could possibly need, and this is key to whatever we would like to do here on the planet. Giving yourself the gift of a clear Crown Chakra will not only help you, but will help all the people you will assist from this place of clarity and grace.

We ask that the Crown Chakra be cleared, aligned, balanced, and strengthened with the highest vibration of Source energy. Recalibrate, harmonize, while continuing to breathe and relax, and stabilize the Crown Chakra at a new, higher frequency.

Imagine now a Golden White light filling up the space around you. This light clears away all that is not you and attracts only the highest vibrations of love and light.

As you breathe, this light penetrates every cell of your body. Light surrounds you, penetrates you, and fills you with a peaceful, loving feeling. You are light; you are love; you are infinite; you are so much more than enough.

Take a deep breath and take in this feeling, the feeling of your true self. You are a beautiful physical being of pure light. Allow this light to expand around you and within you. You are safe and you are loved. You are complete and you are free.

Bring this light fully and completely into your body and allow it to flow into your feet. Feel the energy flowing from the top of your head down your body and into your feet. Feel yourself filling back into your body and occupying every cell.

Really own this physical body. Make it yours. Come back in until you feel completely full and completely at home.

Chapter 19

Remembering You

As you clear out the thoughts, feelings, and beliefs of others, you should have a more relaxed and clear sense of who you truly are.

Explore how your body is feeling.

Does it feel relaxed and open?

Do you feel more free and alive?

If you still feel any fear or restrictions, settle into those areas and bring more awareness and light into them. Any restriction you may feel is usually someone else's energy or belief, or a thought or belief that does not resonate with who you are as a more expansive being. Think of it like a rock in your comfy slipper. It is uncomfortable to have a rock in your slipper; you do not want to have your foot in there when a rock is in there. It hurts to walk around, but once you remove the rock it feels great to wear them again. Clear out all the energy that is not yours and you will feel wonderful in your body again!

CHAPTER 20

Establishing New Patterns

Everything that has come before this moment has given you amazing tools to now go forth into the world and create a beautiful, strong, and vibrant life. All the things you thought were going to break you were actually challenges to teach you about how to come back to yourself. How to come back to love: the love you have for yourself and the love you have for your now more expansive life. Take this time to appreciate how far you have come during this time of reawakening.

Our lessons and challenges can sometimes put us into a trance of unconsciousness. We need to forget who we are in order to believe we are anything less than expansive love, but during this time of self-discovery we awaken to an even deeper sense of our own worth and our own deeper wisdom of what love truly is.

CHAPTER 21

Relapsing

When you are fully clear of your previous partner, you will have a new perspective on life. You will feel more free, light, loving, and open. Around this time, you might think that you can be friends with your ex, and that it can be like it was in the beginning without the baggage. Please give yourself some time on your own so that your brain and body have time to feel what it is like to be out of the relationship for a while. The more dysfunctional the relationship, the more we want to dive back in, because we think that we can do it better this time.

Please consider this. There is a reason why it did not work out with this person, and going backward is going to activate those lessons again. Sometimes we need to go back to a relationship to finally realize that it really is not going to work out and we have done all we could possibly do.

If this happens you can start this program over again, clear your chakras, and re-pattern yourself. I have been through this cycle several times; as soon as I get out of a relationship, I want to go back to it again just to see if I can make it work again from this different perspective.

Going through a cycle two or more times is perfectly okay. I think we repeat the process until we understand how it works. Once we know how things work, we don't need to repeat ourselves. Please don't be hard on yourself if you fall back into the same old patterns. You now have the tools to be able to clear out the energy and re-pattern yourself. This time it will be easier because you will be able to see the old patterns as they come up.

Conclusion

The End Is the Beginning

Congratulations on completing this program. I hope it has helped you on your journey to finding a beautiful new love relationship with yourself, as well as understanding the energy and core beliefs surrounding your relationships with others.

My greatest wish for you is for you to feel grounded, safe, and unconditionally loved by the most important person in your life: YOU.

Be gentle with yourself as you go through the process of remembering you. This life is interesting. It is a series of lessons which make us forgot who we are, so we can have the fun of remembering who we are again. In the process, we become someone who is the same, yet different, somehow—stronger and wiser. Life doesn't have to be hard. It can be whatever we want it to be, and whatever you choose to focus on, that is what you will become.

Focus on Love.
Focus on Joy.

Focus on Freedom.
Focus on Happiness.
Focus on Truth.

And then, focus on all the other wonderful things you want to bring in! Your life is for living!

Make it a good one!

Next Steps

If you would like to do some deeper *Moving On and Letting Go* work, please feel free to go to my website for more audio meditations and video courses.

Best wishes on your unfolding journey of love!

Joanna
www.unfoldinglove.com

Reference List

Abraham Hicks
www.Abraham-Hicks.com

Eckhart Tolle, *The Power of Now*
www.eckharttolle.com

Hands of Light, *Barbara Brennon*
www.barbarabrennan.com

Grounding
www.groundology.com

Dain Heer, *Being You Changing the World*
www.beingyouchangingtheworld.com

Bradley Nelson, *The Emotion Code*
www.healerslibrary.com

Masaru Emoto, *Messeges From Water*
hado.com/ihm/water-crystals/

Mathew Hussey, *How to Get the Guy*
www.matthewhussey.com

Jason Silva
www.thisisjasonsilva.com

Pema Chodron
pemachodronfoundation.org

Nahko
nahko.com

SARK
planetsark.com

Lousie Hay
www.louisehay.com

Marrianne Williamson
marianne.com

Gerald G. Jampolsky
www.ahinternational.org

Lynn Grabhorn
www.amazon.com/Lynn-Grabhorn/e/B001K8IL7U

Wayne Dyer
www.drwaynedyer.com

About the Author

Joanna's life has been a whirlwind of relationships, traveling and living in exotic places such as; the jungles of Belize and Thailand, the islands of Hawaii, the deserts of Africa, forests of Maine and even a monastery on a mountain top just outside of Katmandu in Nepal.

Through it all, she realized that it doesn't matter where you are in the world or what you are doing; if you don't have a strong positive attitude or love for yourself, you could be in the most beautiful place surrounded by daily miracles and you wouldn't be able to see it or feel it.

Through many personal life experiments and lessons, Joanna figured out how tap into Divine Love within and now wants to share that knowledge with others so they can do it too.

Made in the USA
Monee, IL
29 February 2020

22417967R00085